PRAISE FOR BRIAN MCDONALD AND *INVISIBLE INK*

Writing stories is hard. They are stubborn by nature. No matter how many times you master one, the next story is obligated to conceal its faults with an entirely new disguise. Your only recourse is to keep writing, while concurrently increasing your understanding of this deceivingly simple, yet highly complex, organism we call *story*. Brian McDonald's insightful book does just that. Somehow, Brian has found yet another fresh and objective way to analyze how great stories function, and emboldens you to face the challenge of scaling whatever story mountain looms before you. If I manage to reach the summit of my next story it will be in no small part due to having read *Invisible Ink*.

—Andrew Stanton (cowriter of *Toy Story, Toy Story 2, A Bug's Life, Monsters, Inc.,* and cowriter/director of *Finding Nemo* and *WALL-E*)

Invisible Ink is a powerful tool for anyone who wants to become a better screenwriter. With elegance and precision, Brian McDonald uses his deep understanding of story and character to pass on essential truths about dramatic writing. Ignore him at your peril.

—Jim Taylor (Academy Award™- winning screenwriter of *Sideways* and *Election*)

Brian McDonald knows that underneath a good story are the difficult mechanics of plot. He offers insights into both the construction needed and the art of hiding that construction.

—Jim Uhls (screenwriter of *Fight Club*)

Brian McDonald's *Invisible Ink* is a wise, fresh, and highly entertaining book on the art of storytelling. I read it hungrily in one sitting, delighted by his careful and illuminating analysis of my favorite films, novels, television shows, and even comics. A multitalented creator, McDonald never errs in his critical judgments or the very practical principles he provides for creating well-made stories. I recommend this fine handbook on craft to any writer, apprentice or professional, working in any genre or form.

—Dr. Charles Johnson (National Book Award-winning author of *Middle Passage*)

Nobody, in Hollywood or out, understands story better than Brian McDonald. Never give a script to Brian to read casually, because he doesn't know how to do that. He only knows how to make it better— whether you like it or not.

—Mark Handley (screenwriter of *Nell*)

If you want to write scripts, listen to Brian. The guy knows what he's talking about. A very well-thought-out, easy-to-follow guide to the thing all we writers love to pretend we don't slavishly follow—story structure.

—Paul Feig (creator of NBC's *Freaks and Geeks*)

Brian unlocks the secrets to making a great screenplay. I only wish I had read it sooner.

—Steve Higgins (producer, *Saturday Night Live*)

Invisible Ink is an uncommonly good guidebook that reveals the unseen workings within great movies, TV, and literature. Brian McDonald, the author of the guidebook, is like a modern-day magician who understands the enchantment that lives within a good story, and fortunately for us, he is ready to share his many secrets.

—Joel Hodgson (creator of *Mystery Science Theater 3000* and *Cinematic Titanic*)

Storytelling has been my bread and butter for twenty-five years now, and in that time I've sat down with at least a couple of dozen books that swore they could help me with my craft. *Invisible Ink* is the first one I've finished. Brian McDonald understands story like no one else, from the need for and nature of an underlying structure—'armature' is his fine and nimble term for it—through the land-mine-laden path to fleshing it out. McDonald himself is a screenwriter, but this is by no means a book solely for screenwriters. It's not about screenwriting; it's about writing and telling stories. If you're a writer of any kind—fiction, short stories, textbooks, travel articles, newspaper features, you name it—you'll come away from *Invisible Ink* with a deeper grasp of how you do what you do… and how to do it better. And you'll never look at *The Wizard of Oz* in quite the same way again.

—Aaron Elkins (Edgar Award–winning mystery novelist)

Brian McDonald's *Invisible Ink* lays the foundations for storytellers of any kind to do what they are supposed to do: communicate clearly and entertain. Had I not had the good fortune of meeting Brian when I was young, I have no doubt that I would be aimlessly lost in the miasma of ideas, instead of where I am today.

--Brian Kalin O'Connell (episodic director on the animated *Star Wars: Clone Wars*)

The nuts and bolts of storytelling are laid out with clarity, passion, and fun. A lively read, with vivid examples throughout. It's inspiring.

—Paul Chadwick (creator of the critically acclaimed comic book, *Concrete*)

Don't tell anyone, but the secret to exceptional story crafting is written in *Invisible Ink*. I advise you read it, memorize it, and then eat the pages one at a time and digest it thoroughly, so that it stays with you. Besides, you can't afford for this book to fall into the hands of your competitors. Brian's powerful concept of armature as understructure will change the way you look at movies and writing forever.
—Pat Hazell (producer/playwright/former writer for NBC's *Seinfeld*)

Invisible Ink fell into my hands at just the right time—as I was banging my head against the wall trying to structure a screenplay that had too much going on in it. The book's thoughtful exploration of what makes movies work helped me see my core story clearly and throw away a third of my material—which I now understand will not be missed. I have a stronger, more focused script thanks to a process inspired by this book.
—George Wing (screenwriter of *50 First Dates*)

Invisible Ink is a great, easy-to-understand guide to the screenplay writing process. Brian breaks it all down to its simplest form. I found the information the most accessible of any book of this genre. Read it before you start your next script, then read it again when you've finished your first draft.
—Joel Madison (television and film writer/producer)

BRIAN McDONALD

INVISIBLE INK

BUILDING STORIES FROM THE INSIDE OUT

SECOND EDITION

TALKING DRUM

Copyright © 2003, 2005, 2024 Brian McDonald. All Rights Reserved.
Invisible Ink by Brian McDonald is licensed under a Creative Commons Attribution-Noncommercial-No Derivative Works 3.0 United States License.
No part of this book may be used or reproduced in any manner whatsoever without written permission except in the case of brief quotations embodied in critical articles or reviews. Neither the publisher nor the author is engaged in rendering legal or other professional services through this book. If expert assistance is required, the services of an appropriate competent professional should be sought. The author and publisher shall have neither liability nor responsibility to any person or entity with respect to any loss or damage caused, or alleged to have been caused, directly or indirectly by the information contained in this book.

FIRST EDITION: January 2013
SECOND EDITION: July 2024

Published by Talking Drum

Library of Congress Control Number: 2016921321
Cataloging in Publication Data on file with Publisher

Hardcover ISBN: 978-1-7360746-7-1
Paperback ISBN: 978-1-7360746-5-7
Kindle ISBN: 978-1-7360746-6-4

Cover Design: Zac & Kiri Schwiet, Studio Wasaki
Author Photo (back cover): Delilah Lovejoy
Author Photo (About the Author): Ziggy Mack
Publishing and Production: Concierge Marketing Inc.

Printed in the United States of America
10 9 8 7 6 5 4 3 2

STEWART STERN SCREENWRITER OF *REBEL WITHOUT A CAUSE*

Foreword

This is the only book on screenplay structure I have ever had the least inclination to read all the way through. Something has always kept me out of structure books: They seemed too confident to reach for and very unpleasant if you got there. Any semblance of structure in my screenplays has been mainly accidental, relying on emotional tides that often beguiled then drowned me. I love Invisible Ink for inviting me in, for showing me I can touch the stove without burning my hand, and for not holding up to me, as examples to follow, more than one of those overwhelmingly intimidating models, the "3 Cs": Citizen Kane, Chinatown, and Casablanca. Brian McDonald's rich curiosity takes him to different allusions, unexpected literary originals that anyone of courage who had a childhood can climb. Eerily and precisely to the point, they enroll us without threat, not just because they're entertaining in themselves, but because his examples let us hold out our aprons safely to all the trees he plucks them from as we walk with him on the guided tour of his wonderful varied orchard—here Aesop, there nursery rhymes, farther on fairy tales, comic books, cartoons, the Bible, the theater, anthropological discoveries, bar room jokes, Billy Wilder, Shakespeare, Spielberg, Pixar, The Wizard of Oz, ancient African proverbs, and two irreplaceables, Joe Guppy and Matt Smith. With Invisible Ink Brian McDonald has written us a book to keep and heed forever because through the simple, graceful, graspable, original wisdom of it, we might just save our screenwriting lives.

ACKNOWLEDGMENTS

I would very much like to thank my former student Heather for insisting that I write this book. And thanks, also, to Pat who convinced me that I could write this book. And thanks very much to Michael who has been a fan of the book since before it existed. And gratitude to Wayno for always being a cheerleader.

All teachers who write books thank their students, and I am no different. My students have taught me more about my craft than any teacher ever could.

Thanks, too, to my family for celebrating all of our triumphs, great and small.

For Jesse.

If you put a gun onstage in Act I, you must use it by Act III.
—Anton Chekhov

If there is something wrong with the third act, it's really in the first act.
—Billy Wilder

CONTENTS

Foreword vii

Acknowledgments ix

Introduction 1

Chapter I   What is invisible ink? 5

Chapter II   What is a story? 7
    Why do we tell stories? 9
    Stories in their natural habitat exercise 13
    Seven easy steps to a better story 13

Chapter III   The armature 23
    Story is structure—Bones, muscles, and skin 30
    First act breakdown 33
    How to construct a story using armature 41
    Theme beats logic 62
    The use of clones 65

Chapter IV   Charged objects 81
    What is a charged object? 81
    Ritual pain 88
    The power of sacrifice in stories 98
    From butterfly to caterpillar 100
    Killing the protagonist 106

| Chapter V | Tell the truth | 111 |

    Iron and silk: Dual forces that shape compelling narrative 114

    Drama in real life 122

    The myth of genre 124

    Climax 129

    Supporting plots (subplots) 130

    Servant, not master 131

| Chapter VI | Dialogue | 133 |

    Sounding natural 136

    Address and dismiss 137

    Address and explain 138

| Chapter VII | Superior position | 145 |

    Show them once so they know 147

| Chapter VIII | When bad things happen to good stories | 151 |

    How to translate critiques 155

    Judging your own work 156

| Chapter IX | Good stories, good business | 159 |

| Chapter X | My own process | 165 |

    White Face 165

    Tell them what you told them 181

About the Author 185

INTRODUCTION

The world has changed quite a bit since I wrote the original edition of this book. Gender, for example, has become a source of much debate. Consequently, my chapter on the "masculine" and "feminine" elements of story now appears antiquated, even offensive to some. I have attempted to amend that section. However, some other chapter or idea in this edition might be expressed in a way that will not age well. There is little to be done about that.

Another reason for revisiting this book is that I have learned more and I want to delve more deeply into certain ideas. For instance, I will explore the importance of a solid Act One more thoroughly.

Despite this willingness to delve into new depths, I often find myself defending my apparent attachment to the past. In my classes and my books, my examples are often taken from older films, books, television shows, and even comic books. This perceived preference for the "old" frequently comes into question during my corporate engagements. I'm regularly asked to update the film clips I use to demonstrate concepts to something more current—something the audience can identify with, I am told.

To me, this is akin to asking a painting instructor who is teaching the power of single-source lighting to drop his use of Dutch masters such as Vermeer or Rembrandt because their paintings are old.

My reluctance to honor this request is often seen as stubborn, unyielding, or hopelessly nostalgic. Perhaps it is, but I do see a level of craft in the older work that seems to be disappearing. Human beings have lost knowledge before—the secret of Roman concrete, for instance.

It seems to me that the craft of storytelling is in real danger of being lost—or at the very least, deteriorating significantly.

I sometimes work with movie studios that seem to have no idea that there is a craft to storytelling. I was recently told by a producer (in a condescending tone, I might add) that the only method of creating stories is to try things at random to see what sticks. It's no surprise that this studio and others are seeing the quality of their films, the admiration of their audiences, and, of course, the box-office receipts for their films undergoing a steep and steady decline. Yet they stay the course of throwing things at the wall to see what sticks in a fashion akin to outright superstition. They might as well be reading tea leaves or bones.

As I write this, most films are remakes (now marketed as re-imaginings) or sequels, or prequels of things that worked previously. More often than not, these stories are poor forgeries of the masterpieces that spawned them.

Once upon a time, storytelling legends such as Billy Wilder and Rod Serling could churn out one masterpiece after another. Sure, they had their missteps, but they were still able to consistently produce great work.

I suppose one could chalk this up to talent. Talent, by the way, is a terrible word. It does the world no good at all. Talent is something we either have or don't have. It's a trap door that allows us to escape the hard work of mastering our craft. We can shrug and claim we just don't have the talent. But every talented master has hours and hours of hard work under their belt.

One of the Western world's most recognized geniuses, the great composer Mozart, once said, "I assure you, dear friend, nobody has devoted so much time and thought to compositions as I. There is not a famous master whose music I have not industriously studied through many times. I too had to work hard, so as not to have to work hard any longer." Talent, to the extent that it can be said to exist at all, is what hard work looks like from the other side.

What I hope to do with this book is to point you in the right direction so that through your own hard work, you can produce work that others might describe as genius. Only you, I, and Mozart will know the truth.

CHAPTER I

What is Invisible Ink?

"There is no art which does not conceal a still greater art."
– Percival Wilde

A friend of mine once took an anthropology class in which she heard this story:

An anthropologist was living among tribal people with little to no contact with the modern world. Wanting to share the marvels of technology with these isolated folks, the anthropologist took a photo of the chief and his wives. When the picture was processed and shown to the chief, he was unable to recognize the blotches of black, white, and gray as an image of himself. He had never learned to translate two-dimensional images into recognizable three-dimensional shapes. That same chief, however, could look at a patch of grass and say what kind of animal had traversed it and how long ago with no more difficulty than you or I would have recognizing ourselves in a photographic image.

Story structure works in very much the same way. It is easy to see if you know what to look for, but invisible if you don't.

Often when I listen to how people evaluate stories, I hear them talk about dialogue. When they talk about "the script" for a film, they are often talking about the dialogue. Or when they mention how well a book is written, they most often mean the way the words are put together—the beauty of a sentence.

When people speak of Shakespeare's work, they almost always talk about the beauty of the language.

These are all forms of "visible ink." This term refers to writing that is readily "seen" by the reader or viewer, who often mistakes these words on the page as the only writing the storyteller is doing.

But how events in a story are ordered is also writing. Including specific events in a story to make the teller's point is also writing. Why a character behaves in a particular way is also writing.

These are all forms of "invisible ink," so called because they are not easily spotted by a reader, viewer, or listener of a story. Invisible ink does, however, have a profound impact on a story. More to the point, it *is* the story. Invisible ink is the writing below the surface of the words. Most people will never see or notice it, but they will feel it. If you learn to use it, your work will feel polished, professional, and have a profound impact on your audience.

This book teaches you to see the elements that actually constitute *story*, and it shows you how to apply them to your own work. Even stories that you are most familiar with will reveal their inner workings to you in ways you have never seen before.

By the end of this book, you will be able to see footprints in the grass.

CHAPTER II

What Is a Story?

- Why do we tell stories?
- Stories in their natural habitat exercise
- Seven easy steps to a better story

Most people who teach story never bother to define it. This has never made any sense to me. I remember having a friendly, if a bit contentious, argument about a film that I didn't think worked. I was asked what I didn't like about it, and I said that it didn't have a story. The response was, "Well, I think it did."

We could not even agree on what a story was. The problem is that if each of us is walking around with a personal definition of story without realizing it, then we cannot communicate effectively.

One thing I have noticed over the years is that when I talk about stories and storytelling people tend to think of stories in their domesticated form. They think of books or plays or movies or comic books, etc. And when I talk about storytelling they often put it in the context of either tribal storytelling or telling stories to children.

But stories and storytelling exist outside of these forms. There is the feral, untamed story—the stories that we tell every day when we think we are just talking. This is storytelling, too. In fact, it is the parent form of every other kind of storytelling. All of the rules of storytelling can be found in this form. If you really want to learn how stories work, learn to observe them in the wild.

When I began teaching, the very first question I would ask my students is "What is a story?" Usually this question would be met with blank stares. I would let people struggle for uncomfortable minutes as their eyes darted around the room looking for others to answer this oddly difficult question.

What always struck me was that if I had just launched into teaching story without defining it, everyone would have assumed that they knew the definition. This is why I let people ponder the question—because if I had told them right away they would all have shrugged and assumed that they knew it.

Our familiarity with stories creates the illusion that we know more about them than we do. For instance, I have been around cars all my life and have been driving most of my life, and though I am familiar with cars I could not build one. I can't even fix one. I am also quite familiar with houses. I've been in and around houses all of my life—longer than I can remember, in fact. But all of this familiarity does not mean that I would understand how to design one, and it would be ridiculous for me to argue with an architect or builder about the construction of a house.

Story is a place where everyone feels qualified to weigh in, regardless of how little time they have spent studying the topic. Our familiarity with stories creates the illusion of expertise. But when students are asked to simply define a story, the room goes silent.

And even though most of us can't build a car or a house from scratch, we could very easily define those things. But story, which most people cannot even define, is something people feel quite qualified to speak on even with an expert.

In my classes when a brave soul did answer my question, they would say something generic like "A story is a beginning, middle, and end." This, of course, comes from Aristotle's book *Poetics*. Aristotle goes on to clarify just what he means by a beginning, middle, and end. Just to say that a story is a beginning, middle, and end makes very little sense because it is too general. Literally everything in existence fits this definition. Everything from a bus route to the entire universe has a beginning, middle, and end.

As my work has reached a larger audience over the years, some people in my classes now give me an incomplete definition of story that is almost verbatim my definition, but they all claim that they have never heard my definition and it is merely a coincidence that they use my very words.

So what is a story? My definition: A story is the telling or retelling of a series of events leading to a conclusion.

When people are misquoting me, they will often answer "A series of events." This definition is incomplete because it leaves out a teller. A series of events without a teller is not a story.

This answer also leaves out the conclusion. All stories have a reason to be told.

Why does it matter to have a definition for story? I once heard a jazz bassist say that he became a better musician when he looked up the word *bass* in the dictionary. He found that a *base* was a foundation upon which to build. Once he knew that, he understood his role better. His job was to be a foundation for the other musicians to build on. Just having this definition made him better at his job.

Now that we have a shared definition for what a story is, we can begin to talk about how to construct one. Well, almost. I have one more basic question to ask.

WHY DO WE TELL STORIES?

This is another question that induces silence among my pupils. As individuals we might have many reasons to tell stories, but why do we do it as a species? Storytelling is a universal human activity. There has been no culture in world history that has not told stories. So why do we do it?

Think about what ravenous consumers we are of stories.

Answers I sometimes receive are "to entertain, to pass the time, to share experiences, to express ourselves, to connect, to pass on history." And my response is always "Why are those things important?" No matter what answers are offered, this is my response because none of these answers go deep enough.

I then ask people what food is for. The answer that comes back is "So we can live. We need food to live."

Yes. My one-word reason for why we tell stories is survival.

This does not satisfy some of my students because they can think of many other reasons to tell stories. They are not wrong. There are also many reasons to eat. We might eat to mask sadness and to feel comforted. We might eat as part of a ritual such as a holiday or a date. A date is ritualized eating. We might eat out of boredom. None of these things change the core reason for eating food: to survive. The same is true, I believe, with stories.

The fact that there are no people on earth in the history of the world that have *not* told stories indicates that the trait must have been selected for. Like all things selected for, there must have been an advantage to our species in engaging in this activity.

Stories are a way to pass on survival strategies. We also help stories survive. Stories have a memetic quality and can survive themselves as long as they help us survive and navigate the world. We have stories that are thousands of years old. We have stories that have outlasted the civilizations and people that first told them. Sometimes even the original language that these stories were told in is no longer spoken, but we still have the stories. This is because they have value to us still. It helps us to know, for instance, that a wolf sometimes wears sheep's clothing. Or that some things are more valuable than gold. Or, as we learn in the Aesop fable of "The Boy Who Cried Wolf," those known to be liars will not be believed even when they do tell the truth.

By the way, these are the conclusions I was talking about when I defined stories as telling, or retelling, of events leading to a conclusion.

Some students get stuck on the word *survival* and go directly to physical survival, but there are many kinds of survival. There is emotional survival, spiritual survival, cultural survival, and social survival. There may be more, but you get the idea.

Understanding that if you are known to be a liar you will not be believed even when you tell the truth is social survival.

In 12-Step programs such as Alcoholics Anonymous, people attend meetings and share their stories. These stories may contain any or all of the kinds of survival mentioned above. And all of the stories are medicinal in the settings for both teller and listener. Many other types of support groups are also centered around storytelling.

These types of stories are about emotional or spiritual survival. Hearing the story of someone who shares our struggles may give us the boost we need to keep fighting. After all, if they have gotten through it, maybe you can too.

For several years I was part of a program called The Red Badge Project that taught military veterans with post-traumatic stress syndrome how to tell their stories to help with their treatment. When I asked them about what kinds of stories they were told when they were deployed, they told me that there were lots of stories they were told about how to stay alive. These were stories of physical survival in their natural habitat.

I think children gravitate to stories for this very reason. Have you ever seen a group of children when someone announces that it's story time? They become almost giddy with excitement, almost as if they are being fed… which I think they are. Children are new to the world and are trying to figure out how it works. This, I believe, is why stories so often go from older to younger or from more experienced to less experienced. It's why more experienced soldiers have stories for the new recruits.

I often hear from students that stories are for entertainment. Stories are no more for entertainment than food is for tasting good. Food tastes good because nature wants us to eat. My belief is that stories are engaging for this same reason: nature wants us to consume them.

We, as a species, are ravenous consumers of stories. We might listen to a series of news stories on our commute to work, read or listen to a book, listen to a podcast, or ingest stories any number of ways. We go through our day telling and consuming stories in their natural habitat, and then when we want to relax in the evening we look for a story to watch. Then we go to sleep and enter a story world even while we are unconscious and are dreaming.

Another clue to storytelling being linked to survival is that every writing teacher will tell you that stories must have conflict. Why? Some instructors will say because it makes stories more interesting. Again, I ask why? It's because conflict is the thing we are trying to survive.

If you ever come across a story that doesn't seem to be about survival, look deeper; you may find you haven't looked closely enough.

Just knowing that this is the purpose of storytelling will improve your work.

Later in this book I will address how you pass on this kind of information without being preachy or heavy-handed.

STORIES IN THEIR NATURAL HABITAT EXERCISE

1. For the next week, or as long as you would like, become an active listener during conversations. Listen to the stories people tell when they think they are just talking. Try to notice how often we tell stories in our daily lives.
2. You can keep a journal, if you like, of the stories that you hear. See if you can figure out what kind of survival information is embedded in the story. Does the story involve emotional, physical, cultural, social, or spiritual survival?
3. Try to pay attention to the stories you yourself tell to others and what kinds of survival information you are giving to your listeners.

SEVEN EASY STEPS TO A BETTER STORY

Stories are not complicated. They are, in fact, deceptively simple. But like anything simple, they are difficult to create. I realize that sounds a little like Lewis Carroll, but hear me out.

One of the things that hangs us all up when writing is that we feel we need to make it more complicated than it is. We feel that this will make it better, but it never does. It just makes it muddy.

I often hear people say, "less is more." But I don't see it reflected in their work. What follows are seven steps that make up all narratives. I was taught them by a writer/teacher by the name of Matt Smith. He learned them from a guy named Joe Guppy. And you are learning them from me.

Here are the steps:

1. Once upon a time
2. And every day
3. Until one day
4. And because of this
5. And because of this
6. Until finally
7. And ever since that day

These steps are a kind of invisible ink. I'm sure you recognize them. They just make sense, don't they? Why didn't you know them already? You did. You just thought it would be more complicated than that.

Once upon a time... and every day...

There are many books you can read that explain three-act structure, so I will cover it only briefly here using the seven steps as a template.

Let's look at the first two steps: "Once upon a time" and "And every day." They are your Act One. What is the purpose of Act One? It tells the audience everything they need to know to understand the story that is to follow.

Let's look at what legendary filmmaker Billy Wilder says about the importance of a good first act: "If there is something wrong with the third act, it's really in the first act." Most of us have no problem understanding the importance of the first act of a joke. When someone tells a joke poorly, it is more likely than not that they have forgotten to convey an important piece of information in the set-up that makes the punch line funny. So it seems the joke is in the set-up and not the punch line.

Just as with a joke, a story's set-up must tell the audience everything they need to know to understand the story.

What does an audience need to know? Think of your childhood storybooks: Once upon a time there were Three Bears who lived together in their own house in the forest: Mama Bear, Papa Bear, and Baby Bear. They each had a bowl for their porridge—a small bowl for Baby Bear, a middle-sized bowl for Mama Bear, and a big bowl for Papa Bear.

We know several things just from those few sentences. Yes, we know there are three bears. We know that there are at least three major characters and we know their relationship to one another. But we also know that these bears behave like people. That is important. You could very well have a story where the bears act like animals.

Remember, when you create a story, you must let the audience know the reality of your story. It's your world.

"A duck walks into a bar and orders a rum and Coke." That joke starts by giving you a major character and letting you know the reality. Notice that when a joke starts with a duck walking into a bar, no one says, "That's ridiculous!" They accept it because it's the first thing they are told. Whatever your "talking duck" is, let people know right away.

The opening of *Raiders of the Lost Ark* is often talked about because it's exciting. But it is much more than that. With so many fantastical things happening right at the story's opening, the audience knows a few things about its world. We know that the story's reality is heightened—that it is not to be a story about a soldier coping with his life after Vietnam. It is a fantasy that takes place in the year 1936. We know that in this world, archaeology is much more than just digging for pieces of clay pots. We know, also, that the guy in the fedora is good with a whip and good at his job. He appears to be fearless and smart. Things don't always go as planned for him, and he sometimes survives by the skin of his teeth.

We meet Belloq, Indiana Jones's archenemy, so we know his is a ruthless business, and men will kill for the valuable artifacts they seek.

We see that Indiana Jones fears snakes. He's not superhuman.

Which brings up something else. We know some things because they are defined by their absence. We know that Indiana Jones may be skilled, but he does not possess magical powers. In some realities, magical powers are commonplace, but not in this one. There is another Spielberg film that shows what a disaster it can be to have a poor first act: In the mid-1980s, Steven Spielberg produced a television show called *Amazing Stories*. A particular episode, "The Mission," was one Mr. Spielberg also directed.

The story takes place during WWII, aboard a B-17 bomber. B-17s had a crew of ten. One of the crewmen was positioned under the belly of the plane in a Plexiglass bubble so he could fire his machine gun at any threat coming from underneath the plane.

In this story, the "belly-gunner" is a talented and likable guy who draws caricatures of his crewmates, much to their amusement. He wants to work for Walt Disney Studios.

The plane goes on a bombing mission and is badly damaged. When the belly-gunner tries to crawl out of his bubble and into the plane, he finds that he is trapped underneath the plane because of the damage.

The crew tries to get him out, but they can't. No problem—they can just get him out when they land. Then someone suggests that they check the landing gear, and they find out that it doesn't work. Without wheels, the plane will have to land on its belly, crushing the helpless gunner to death.

The crew does not want to give up on their buddy and increases the effort to save him. Nothing works.

Certain that the man will die, the airbase calls a priest to be there when the plane lands.

It becomes painfully clear that the belly-gunner is going to die and nothing can be done to prevent it. Each of the crew members puts his hand down the small top opening of the bubble to say goodbye. They are in tears as they rub the gunner's head or embrace his hand.

Without the belly-gunner's knowledge, the decision has been made to shoot him so that he won't suffer the pain of being crushed.

Slowly, one of the men pulls his pistol and lowers it down to the head of his unsuspecting friend.

The poor gunner is crying and muttering that he can't die because he's going to work for Walt Disney Studios.

The pistol creeps ever closer to his head as he busily sketches a cartoon version of a B-17. He is almost in a trance. He draws big, cartoonish wheels on the bottom of the plane.

As they approach the landing strip, the pilot decides to try one last time to lower the landing gear. His indicators tell him that the wheels have lowered.

From the bottom of the real plane, big, exaggerated cartoon tires emerge. They make the sound of a squeaky balloon and are complete with a cartoon tire patch. The plane is able to land on these cartoon tires, and the man is saved.

The night this show aired, I had a group of friends over to watch the show. I can tell you that we were riveted to the screen during this show. We kept wondering how the hell they were going to get out of this. The tension and suspense were palpable.

We all reacted with disappointed laughter upon the landing of the plane on cartoon wheels. So, it turns out, did the rest of America.

I can't tell you how disappointed audiences were when this episode aired. I remember how, the next day, people at work talked about how bad it was. They thought the entire episode was awful.

Spielberg had not set up a reality where cartoon tires could save the day. There are realities in which this would have been possible: *Who Framed Roger Rabbit*, for example.

Spielberg had done such a good job with the first part of the story that we, the audience, believed the situation was dire. We were invested in the story and its world. The cartoon tires were from some other world we knew nothing about.

Just as Billy Wilder said, "If there is something wrong with the third act, it's really in the first act," so your "Once upon a time" is the reality in which your story takes place and the introduction of your major characters.

"And every day…" just supports what has already been set up. It establishes a pattern. A pattern to be broken by…

Until one day…

An inciting incident occurs. The inciting incident is the true beginning of your story. If your story is about a couple who has an affair, this might be when they meet. Or if they have already met, it is when the affair begins.

Some will tell you that this is where your conflict begins, but that is not necessarily true. Comic-book writer and editor Jim Shooter has observed that the second act can start with conflict or opportunity. For instance, if you've got a story where the first act is about a young woman who is so poor she can't pay her rent, the first act might end when she finds one million dollars.

This step has been called many things: act break, plot point, turning point, and curtain. I prefer curtain. The reason I like the term *curtain* is because it comes from theater, wherein a curtain is literally dropped between acts. In live theater, they must get the audience back after intermission, so acts end on the highest point, when the stakes are at their most desperate. For me, imagining that there is a physical curtain helps me to remember to raise the stakes.

In his book, *Comedy Writing Step by Step*, comedy writer Gene Perret calls this the "Uh-oh factor." In a well-constructed sketch, the character and/or situation is established and then something happens that requires a reaction. He uses an example from the old Carol Burnett Show in which Carol plays a woman who has just been released from a hospital psych ward where she was treated for her addiction to soap operas. She proclaims that she is cured. She says, "I don't care if Bruce marries Wanda or not." Her friend's response is "Bruce is dead." As Mr. Perret describes it, Carol's eyes widen at this news and the audience thinks, "Uh-oh, she's hooked on soaps again."

Drama has this "uh-oh" moment as well. In Shakespeare's *King Lear*, the king promises his entire fortune to the daughter who can prove she loves him most. That's an "uh-oh" moment if there ever was one.

Few people could stop watching a drama after something like that is introduced.

And because of this…

This is now your second act. When your first "curtain" goes down, that is the end of your first act. Now it is time to explore what happens as a result of your first act—everything should be cause-and-effect. If your character was diagnosed with inoperable cancer at the end of Act 1, this is where he deals with it. Does he go into denial? Does he give up, lie down, and wait to die? Or is he a fighter? Will he try anything for another few days of life? Does he question how he has lived his life and try to do something worthwhile before he dies?

Whatever the character does, it must be in reaction to the incident at the Act 1 curtain.

And because of this...

Act 2 is your longest act and makes up the body of your story. This act is usually split in two. I like to call this split the fulcrum. Because Act 2 is so long, it can be difficult to keep an audience engrossed. It helps to cut it in half.

In Billy Wilder's classic noir film, *Double Indemnity,* a woman and her lover decide to kill the woman's husband for the insurance money. In the first half of Act 2 they plan the murder. At the fulcrum, they carry out their plan, and in the second half of Act 2 the focus becomes: Will they get away with this crime?

Back to our character who was diagnosed with cancer. Let's say that when given the news of his cancer, he gives up on life and begins alienating those who care for him. But at the fulcrum something happens that makes him want to live. Now he will stop at nothing to find a cure.

Until finally...

This is your third act. When the Act 3 curtain "goes up," it is the beginning of the end of the story. In a cop drama, for instance, it might be the clue that solves the big mystery and puts the detective on the trail of the killer. This event, whatever it is, starts the chain of events that leads to your climax.

Using our example of the cancer patient, perhaps this is where he makes peace with the inevitable and accepts his impending death. Perhaps he decides to cherish the moments he has left with family and friends and spends his time with them instead of searching for the elusive cure for his disease.

And ever since that day...

Following your climax is a short scene or two called a denouement. "They lived happily ever after" is the most familiar denouement. You shouldn't have too much following your climax, just something that lets the audience know what the life of your protagonist is like after it.

In the case of our unfortunate cancer patient, he does not survive; but maybe this is where we see how his courage in the face of death has had a lasting impact on those who survive. Or maybe how he lives on through his art. Or perhaps his death has ended old rivalries and caused others to cherish those around them.

What I would like you to do now is write down each of these steps, followed by a blank space. Then I want you to write a few simple stories using these steps. Make them as simple as possible.

What you will find is that what you have written feels like a story, but it seems to lack something. They are shallow for some reason. Forgettable. It is a small matter to fix: all you need to do is have a point.

CHAPTER III

The Armature

- Story is structure—Bones, muscles, and skin
- First act breakdown
- How to construct a story using armature
- What it means to dramatize an idea
- Theme beats logic
- The use of clones

*A wise man speaks because he has something to say; a fool
because he has to say something.*
—*Unknown author; often attributed to Plato*

Why do people tell stories? The stories that tend to stick to our bones are those that teach us something. This, I believe, is the primary reason we tell stories—to teach.

Consider this: Every culture on the globe has music and stories. We all have music, and we all have stories.

People who study human speech believe that humans did not invent language any more than birds invented flight. It is in our makeup to speak. It is part of being human.

It makes sense to me that stories fall under this category. They are part of us. I've seen memory experts on television who will give volunteers a huge list of objects to memorize. Of course, this is difficult to do. Then they tell the volunteer to string the objects together in an absurd story. When this is done, the list is easily recalled. Our brains seem to retain information this way.

I have read about aboriginal tribes in Australia who use songs and stories in case they get lost. These songs contain information like a map. So if you know the words to a particular song, you can, for instance, find water in an unfamiliar area because you know the song for that area.

Besides saving lives, stories can also tell us how we should live.

In Africa, they used to tell the story of a black slave-catcher who helped the English capture his own countrymen and sell them into a life of slavery. One night, after a particularly good catch, the black slave-catcher was celebrating with the English and they all got drunk on rum. The black man passed out, and when he awoke the next day, he found himself in the belly of a slave ship chained to the very people he had helped enslave.

This is a cautionary tale that teaches its listener that there is a price to be paid for betrayal.

In Bruno Bettelheim's book, *The Uses of Enchantment: The Meaning and Importance of Fairy Tales,* he describes the traditional Hindi medical practice of giving the patient a story to contemplate. Through this story the patient would learn from the hero's failures and victories how to deal with and resolve his/her own problem.

This may sound like a foreign concept, but we use it today in Western culture in the form of Alcoholics Anonymous and other 12-Step programs where people share their stories to help themselves and others. This simple act of sharing stories helps the healing process. People learn that they are not alone in their struggle and that others have been through these addictions and survived.

They may also learn things to watch out for in their own behavior to avoid falling back into old destructive patterns.

Stories teach us how to live.

Take the story of King Midas. This man was so greedy that he wished all he touched would turn to gold. That is, until he touched his beloved daughter and she was changed to gold. We learn that some things are more important than money. Like the aboriginal song, this story is a map—a map for living.

Look at the Bible. It could be just a list of rules, but it's not—it's a collection of stories. Stories resonate with people. Lists do not.

If you want people to hold fast to their faith no matter what, you tell them the story of Job. Job would not renounce God, no matter what the Devil did to him, and in the end he was rewarded.

If you want people to stand up to power, no matter what the odds, tell them the story of David and Goliath.

If you want to teach people not to get too full of themselves, you tell them the story of King Nimrod, who thought himself so great that he tried to build a tower to God. He was put in his place when God gave all the workers different languages so they could not communicate.

The Greeks and Romans had similar stories. All religions have understood, for a very long time, that stories are powerful tools. Why is it that some stories stick with us, while others are soon forgotten? Do you remember the story I told you about the tribal chief and the anthropologist? Sure you do. Why? It's because I had a point, a reason to tell that story. Having a point gives your stories resonance. Recall the saying, "A wise man speaks because he has something to say; a fool because he has to say something." This is true when one is crafting a story as well.

Because of my work at make-up effects houses, I've known a few sculptors. When they begin sculpting in clay, they first build an armature to act as a skeleton; otherwise, the piece would not hold its shape. It might look good for a while but would soon collapse. When an admirer of art looks at a sculpture, she never sees or even thinks about the armature that gives the piece its structural integrity. The armature is invisible but as much a part of the sculpture as the outside.

Before you begin writing, you too must build an armature. For us story-crafters, the armature is the idea upon which we hang our story. It is what has been called theme, but I find that the word *theme* is not descriptive enough and leads to confusion; I have found in teaching that many people bring a lot of baggage to the table when I address theme.

What is an armature, then, when talking about story craft? It is what you want to say with your piece. I was once talking to a friend who was complaining about a producer wanting to change a scene in his script. My friend was angry because the change had nothing to do with his theme. He said, "My theme is competition. And the change has nothing to do with competition!" I didn't say anything at the time, but my friend was confused. There is an old joke about marriage that goes, "Marriage is not a word, it's a sentence." It's the same with theme. My friend had nothing to say about competition. "Competition" is not a theme. A theme (or armature) might be "Competition is sometimes a necessary evil." Or "Competition leads to self-destruction." Saying that your theme is competition is like saying your theme is "red." It really says nothing at all.

One way to look at your armature is to find what is called, in children's fables, "the moral." The armature is your point. Your story is sculpted around this point.

With King Midas, the storyteller wanted to teach people that some things were more important than money. What were his tasks as a writer? First, he had to create a character who was greedy.

Then he needed to set up a situation wherein the character gets what he wants. Then he needed to turn this wish into something that would teach the character a lesson. Everything in this story is designed to make the writer's point. This should be true of your work as well.

You may think this definition of theme is too simplistic. It must be harder than this, you think. It isn't. You may also be worried about being perceived as too preachy. Over the years, I have encountered many students concerned with being too preachy or blatant, but never one who was afraid of not being clear enough or that their point would not be understood.

The first thing you must do to get your point across is to understand what you want to say. I know that sounds simple and obvious, but I almost never meet writers who know what they want to say. Mostly what they want is to say something deep and profound that no one has ever said before, but they don't know what that is. Or they want to say a thousand things in one story, not realizing that to say too much is to say nothing at all.

I was once reading an interview with animation director Chuck Jones in which he talked about animating young animals versus old animals. He had observed that a puppy, for instance, would expend excess energy to perform simple tasks. This results in those floppy movements we associate with young mammals. In contrast, adult animals are more economical. Think of the clumsy hunting style of a kitten versus the precision of an adult cat. I have noticed this same thing with story crafters. Writers with the least experience and skill think that the more complicated something is, the better. But like a kitten, their work comes off clumsy and unfocused. If you want to come off like a mature writer, be precise.

The following piece of advice is often given to someone about to give a speech: "Tell them what you're going to tell them. Tell them. Tell them what you told them." This is no different for storytellers. In fact, those three bits of advice could represent the three acts. But just how do you put this into practice? How is your armature put together?

First, you must know where you are going or you will never get there. Then you must let the audience know where you are taking them. You show them the armature—the idea you want to build on. One way to do this is to have a character state out loud what you want to say with your story.

In *E.T.: The Extra-Terrestrial*, when Elliott says something hurtful to his mother, Elliott's older brother gets angry at his insensitivity and yells, "Damn it, when are you going to grow up and learn how other people feel for a change?" What happens next is that Elliott meets E.T. And one of the first things that happens is that when E.T. becomes sleepy, so does Elliott. Then when E.T. is hungry, so is Elliott. When E.T. drinks beer, Elliott gets drunk, too.

Later, when Elliott introduces E.T. to his brother, he says, "I'm keeping him." He has made this decision without any regard for what E.T. wants. But he is beginning to empathize with others, as is evidenced in the scene in which Elliott feels for the frogs in his science class and sets them free before they can be dissected. By the end of the film, Elliott "feels what other people feel" enough to send E.T. home even though he will miss his friend. Everything in the film is built on the armature stated by Elliott's brother at the beginning of the story.

The Iron Giant is an amazing animated film directed by Brad Bird. On its surface, this film is like *E.T.* in many ways. It is about a boy who befriends a being from outer space (in this case, a giant robot). And, as in *E.T.*, the government is seeking the alien. So what's different about it, you might ask. It's the armature. As a matter of fact, I have heard very few people compare the two films.

They each had something different to say, so the similar stuff on the surface didn't matter much.

In the story of *The Iron Giant*, the robot is damaged when it lands on Earth. Later, after befriending the boy, the kindly robot remembers that it is programmed to be a weapon of mass destruction. In fact, it nearly vaporizes the boy by accident. Now the robot has an internal conflict. Will it give in to its programming (its nature) or rise above it? I understand that when Mr. Bird pitched the story, he said, "What if a gun had a conscience and didn't want to be a gun anymore?" That was his armature. In the film it is stated this way: "You are who you choose to be."

I don't believe that audiences care much about the genre of a story; they just want to be moved in some way. And they respond over and over again to stories with an armature.

A film like James Cameron's *Terminator* would seem, on its surface, to have a flimsy armature, but it really has something meaningful to say. If you recall, Sarah Conner was an ordinary 20th-century woman with a stressful low-wage job at a burger joint. In the first act of the film, Sarah is having a particularly bad day at work when her coworker says to her, "Look at it this way: in a hundred years, who will care?"

As it turns out, Sarah's life is about to be turned upside down. A robot from the future has been sent back in time to kill her, to prevent her from giving birth to her son, who is a threat to Skynet (the computer that rules the future Earth). She is, according to the film, one of the most important people ever born. So this mundane life that she lives does, indeed, matter. In a hundred years, everyone will care who Sarah Connor was.

This is not unlike *It's a Wonderful Life*, wherein George Bailey thinks it would make little difference to the world if he had never been born. He learns, of course, that his life has had a great impact on the people around him, and even on some he has never met.

On the surface these two movies would seem to have nothing in common, but they share a common armature: none of us knows how important our mundane life may prove to be.

Yes, these are all high-key fantasy films, but armature also applies to straight dramas. They can also state their armature out loud. In *Kramer vs. Kramer*, a story in which Dustin Hoffman's wife, played by Meryl Streep, walks out on him and leaves him with their child, Dustin is speaking with a neighbor who tells him that what Meryl did took a lot of courage. His response is: "Oh, yeah, how much courage does it take to walk out on your child?" By the end of the film, that question is answered for Dustin and for the audience. Watch it and see.

In *The Wizard of Oz* the armature is stated: "There's no place like home." But it might more accurately be said: "You may already have what you are looking for." How do we know that this is so? Is it because it is said? No, it's because it is dramatized.

Remember that your armature is the foundation that holds up your story. Everything hangs on top of it. Every decision you make should be based on the idea of dramatizing your armature idea.

STORY IS STRUCTURE—BONES, MUSCLES, AND SKIN

> *"It is the pervading law of all things organic and inorganic, that form ever follows function."*
> — Louis Sullivan

Story structure is often debated. People have different opinions about what makes good story structure and what doesn't, for instance. There are also those who believe that stories don't need a structure at all. My belief is that stories are not simply guided by structure; they are themselves structures. Just as a building or a bridge is a structure, so too is a story. Without structure, a story would amount to a series of unconnected events. Once one connects these events to give them collective meaning, they become pieces of a whole—they become a story. That is structure.

It was a playwright who once pointed out to me the curious construction of the word *playwright*. The term originates from the Old English word *wright*, meaning "builder." A shipwright, for example, is a builder of ships. Thus, we who create stories are builders of story. As builders, we have much to learn from other types of construction.

Understanding the purpose or function of the structure you are building is the first step. For instance, are you constructing a pedestrian walkway over a freeway, or a bridge designed to carry heavy traffic over a large body of water? Similarly, you need to know the purpose of the building you are designing. Is it a single-family home, a 76-story office building, or a wedding chapel? This principle—form follows function—dictates your structural choices.

The function of a story is its point—its armature. Understanding the purpose of the story you want to tell will guide the design and construction of that story. As Steve Jobs aptly put it, "Design is not just what it looks like and feels like. Design is how it works."

"Form follows function" is not a new concept. Louis Sullivan, regarded as the father of modernism in architecture, coined the phrase "form ever follows function." This principle is also evident in nature, where the form of each part of a natural system reflects its function. Consider the Orca whale: its black-and-white coloration is not merely aesthetic but serves a functional purpose, making it difficult for both prey and predators to spot them.

So, how do you go about constructing your story? The process is somewhat similar to building anything else—from the inside out: bones, muscles, skin.

Bones: The foundational structure

The "bones" of your story provide the foundational structure, akin to the skeleton in an anatomical body or an architect's blueprint for a building. This is where you sketch out your core idea. This step should be loose and not too detailed. Overcomplicating this stage can lead to procrastination, halting progress.

Muscles: The details

The muscle layer is where you work out the story's logistics and flesh out character details. For instance, if your foundational structure includes a plot point where Character A discovers that her business partner is embezzling money, the muscle stage is where you detail exactly how this unfolds.

Skin: The outer layer

The skin is the finishing touch, the aesthetic elements like word choice, style, and tone that form the immediate experience for your audience.

Most people don't marvel at a building's foundation or frame; they appreciate its visual and functional design. The same is true for stories. Your audience may not explicitly recognize the foundational structure, but they will feel its stability and effectiveness.

This "bones, muscles, skin" framework is particularly useful for collaborations. When everyone knows what layer they're working on, the project stays focused and efficient.

Rod Serling, the six-time Emmy-award-winning screenwriter and creator of the classic *Twilight Zone* television series, approached his storytelling this way: "Overall theme leads to character, then on to plot." He started with the theme, or armature, and built his stories layer by layer, just as I am advocating here.

In the realm of storytelling, much like in architecture or anatomy, it's what lies beneath that holds everything together. "Bones, muscles, and skin" is more than a metaphor; it's a way of conceptualizing the invisible architecture that supports every memorable tale. It's a methodology that adds layers to your craft, much like the layers of a building or the anatomy of a living being. And just as you wouldn't appreciate a building solely for its outer layer of paint, a story shouldn't be valued only for its surface-level prose or dialogue. Underneath it all is the structure—the invisible ink—that dictates form, function, and ultimately, impact. As you move forward in your storytelling journey, I challenge you to apply this layered approach. Map out your bones, build your muscles, and then (and only then) apply the skin. Use your invisible ink wisely; it's the writing beneath the words that transforms mere text into a timeless story.

FIRST ACT BREAKDOWN

Having given you an overview of story construction in the previous chapter and in this one, now I would like to zero in on the all-important first act.

At the time of this writing, the first act has fallen out of fashion. I was once told by my short-lived agent not to write a first act for my screenplays. He wanted to get right to the action because, for him, all of the set-up was wasted time.

Then there are those who have read a screenwriting book or two that states that the first act ends on this page or that. So what these writers do is kill time for twenty-five pages or so and then get into the action. But first acts are not about killing time.

So how does a first act function, and why is it necessary?

The first act creates context. It builds rapport between the protagonist and the audience. It lets the audience know the rules of the world and exactly what kind of story is going to be told. It may set up a character's flaw or at least explain enough about the character and her outlook on the world that we will understand how her world has shifted at the end of the act.

It also establishes what the story is about thematically. What is the armature? And why is this character in this story?

This last question is one I ask a lot. I will often watch a movie and ask myself why this character had to be in this story. Why did this character need these events to happen to them for them to change?

When I was a teenager, I received the best writing advice I've ever gotten from a comic book writer by the name of Steve Englehart. He said, "If you've got a Batman story and you can make it into a Superman story, it's not a good Batman story."

What he was saying was that characters are crafted along with the story, so they are unified. If they are not unified and you can pluck out your protagonist and put another protagonist in, your story probably isn't working.

One of the things that happens in your first act is that you're letting the audience know whether this is Superman or Batman. Or you're letting them know that this is Ebenezer Scrooge, and he is miserly. Or you're letting the audience know, as in *E.T. The Extraterrestrial*, that Elliott is a little boy who is sometimes mean to his mother.

I will delve more into the process of building stories based around an armature later, but you will see how Act 1 is constructed around your armature.

Let's take a look at the film *Cast Away*.

I have written about this before, but it's worth including here to help make the point and it's not a crime to plagiarize myself.

Cast Away: Act 1 Breakdown

The film starts with a thematic opening image that captures isolation, loneliness, and emptiness. A solitary FedEx truck, dwarfed in the frame, arrives at an intersection—a symbolic crossroads, much like the one in Chuck Noland's life. (Note the name: No Land.)

This level of precision, being on-the-nose, is something amateurs often avoid. However, effective storytellers relish the opportunity to communicate clearly. As Billy Wilder said, "Don't be too clever for an audience. Make it obvious. Make the subtleties obvious also."

Back in 2000, some people complained that *Cast Away* seemed like an extended FedEx commercial. Yet, Chuck's job at FedEx is integral to the story. When we first meet Chuck, he's lecturing Russian FedEx employees about the importance of time:

"Time rules over us without mercy—not caring if we are healthy or ill, hungry or drunk, Russian, American, or beings from Mars. Time is like a fire—it can either destroy us or keep us warm. That's why every FedEx office has a clock. Because we live or die by the clock. We never turn our back on it. And we never, ever allow ourselves the sin of losing track of time."

In Act 1, Chuck is a man obsessed with time, yet ironically, he doesn't make time for his own life. Always in a rush, he neglects to get the contact information of a doctor who could help a friend's wife with her cancer. It's not that he's indifferent; he just thinks there's plenty of time for everything.

Similarly, Chuck barely has moments to spare for his long-time girlfriend, Kelly. When he does find the time, he's too exhausted from work and falls asleep, thereby committing the sin of "losing time."

At a family dinner, it's an ongoing joke that Chuck has been slow to propose to Kelly. He's so preoccupied with time that he even clocks how long it takes for the subject of marriage to come up—14 minutes, according to his watch.

Though constantly on call, Chuck ignores a lingering dental issue, another task he never gets around to addressing.

His work commitment becomes painfully clear when he's called away from Christmas dinner, much to Kelly's disappointment. Dropping him off at the airport for yet another work trip, Kelly receives a small Christmas box from Chuck—likely an engagement ring. Yet, Chuck stops short of proposing and asks her to open it on New Year's Eve. After a quick kiss, he boards the plane, essentially turning his back on time.

It's worth noting the thematic precision here: Kelly's gift to Chuck is a pocket watch with her picture inside, linking time and love in one powerful image.

The first act culminates in a plane crash that leaves Chuck stranded on a deserted island. He pulls out his waterlogged pager—it's broken. The man who once had no time now has nothing but time. End of Act 1.

In the second act, it becomes clear that Chuck's love for Kelly—his desire to return to her—keeps him alive. He now realizes how he should have spent his time.

There is an exchange later in the film between Chuck and his friend whose wife had cancer and has died while Chuck was stranded on the island. When Chuck is told by the friend that his wife has died, his response is, "I should have been there."

On the surface this makes no sense because of course he could not have been there. But what Chuck is really saying is that he should have made time for the important things.

The first act of *Cast Away* sets up everything that follows, eliciting emotion from the audience. Screenwriter William Broyles, Jr. sends a compelling message: Time is both precious and fleeting. We should never turn our backs on it, and we must never commit the sin of losing time.

Cast Away is full of invisible ink, and that helped make it a hit and a classic.

Finding Nemo: Act 1 Breakdown

Pixar's classic *Finding Nemo* has an amazing first act.

Nemo opens with a beautiful shot under the ocean. This is great because later the ocean will be a scary place, so this contrast is excellent.

The protagonist, Marlin, is with his wife, Coral, and they are very happy with their new home—a sea anemone.

Marlin enthusiastically swims out of the anemone and states, "A fish can really breathe out here!" Again, the open ocean will soon become a frightening place for Marlin, so this contrast helps to clearly illustrate his later change.

Coral says the neighborhood is awesome. We are shown a fun ocean environment full of colorful, happy fish living their best fishy lives.

Soon, Coral and Marlin turn their attention to their kids—400 unhatched fish eggs, their children.

Marlin wants to name half of them Marlin Junior and the other half Coral Junior, but Coral likes the name Nemo. Marlin is not too sure about the name but reluctantly agrees to name one of them Nemo.

Marlin is worried that none of their 400 children will like him, but Coral reassures him that one of them is bound to like him.

This detail matters. Everything matters.

Soon, a toothy barracuda fish attacks the couple, and Marlin is knocked unconscious. When he wakes up, he finds that his wife is gone. Dead.

Marlin is distraught. He then finds that one of the eggs survived the attack. He gently picks up the egg in his fins and promises the unhatched child that he will never let anything bad happen to him. He calls the child Nemo.

Even within the opening, we have a set-up and a payoff with the name of the child. Marlin agreed to name one of the children Nemo, and when there is only one left, he names him Nemo.

This tribute to his dead wife closes the loop. There is an emotional satisfaction when this sort of loop is closed. It makes pieces feel cohesive—like every piece is part of a unified whole.

The film jumps in time to when Nemo is older and is enthusiastic about his first day of school. He swims out of the anemone with gusto, mirroring Marlin in the film's opening.

This is when we see that Marlin is being an overprotective father. He's scared that he might lose Nemo, so he is hyper-vigilant. The ocean is a dangerous place, as we have seen. It's also a beautiful place, as we also have seen. Marlin has forgotten this in his trauma.

We are now introduced to Nemo's "lucky fin." He has an underdeveloped fin—it is smaller than the other. This is further justification for Marlin's vigilance.

Marlin's overprotectiveness will drive a wedge in his relationship with his son, but at this point, we see that they are getting along well. They love each other, though we can see that Nemo is slightly annoyed.

On the way to school, Nemo fires off questions. He asks his father if he's ever seen a shark. "No, and I don't plan to," answers Marlin.

Nemo then wants to know how long sea turtles live. Marlin sarcastically answers that if he ever meets a sea turtle, he'll ask him.

If you know the film, you know that Marlin does later meet both a shark and a sea turtle.

All the way to school, Marlin is his overprotective self as he maneuvers to keep his son out of danger.

At school, Nemo meets classmates who are free to have fun, while his father keeps him close, stifling his chance to have fun with the other kids.

Marlin has a hard time letting go and won't leave when it's time for school. Nemo even asks his father to leave.

But Marlin is brave and says goodbye as Nemo's teacher takes the kids on a field trip. That is, until he finds out where they are going—the drop-off. It's clear that Marlin feels this is a dangerous place, and he sets off to retrieve Nemo.

Nemo enjoys his time alone with his classmates as he takes in the wonders of the ocean.

Nemo and a few new friends secretly sneak off from the teacher and the rest of the group to look at the drop-off. It's like a cliff that leads to the wide-open sea.

Something in the distance catches their attention—the bottom of a boat floating on the surface. They dare each other to get close to the boat. Each takes a turn going further into the ocean and closer to the boat. Nemo stays behind at the edge of the drop-off, even when he is egged on by his buddies, because his dad told him the drop-off was unsafe.

Just then, Marlin arrives on the scene and accuses Nemo of trying to swim into the ocean. He doesn't let Nemo explain himself, and the two have an argument.

Frustrated, Nemo says to his dad, "I hate you." This hits Marlin like a dart in his heart. If you recall Marlin's discussion with Coral, he was concerned that his children would not like him. Coral reassured him that with 400 children, one of them was bound to like him. And now, the only child he has left says he hates him.

This strikes an emotional chord with the audience because this was set up earlier. The line would mean very little without the set-up. We would understand it intellectually but not feel it emotionally.

Defiant, Nemo swims way out into the ocean, and despite his father's protests, he touches the bottom of the boat.

While Nemo is out there, he is scooped up by a diver and taken away.

This is Marlin's worst nightmare. It is also very close to the end of Act 1.

I would call the true end of Act 1 the scene when Marlin meets Dory, his traveling companion on his search for Nemo, and the two come face-to-face with a massive shark who appears to be nothing but teeth.

What did Marlin say when asked if he'd ever seen a shark?

"No, and I don't plan to."

Marlin must now face his fears to find his son.

Everything in Act 1 is there to set the stage for what will follow. It also creates an emotional connection with the characters. We care about Marlin and Nemo, and we care what happens to them. This is the strength of a focused Act 1.

A strong, focused first act is one of the most powerful forms of invisible ink and one of the most important. Without it, a story is nothing more than a series of events strung together. The lack of a first act makes a story hollow, cold, emotionless, and pointless.

Having a strong first act may not seem like a form of invisible ink, but given how many professional storytellers ignore its importance I would say that its power is invisible to many. Learn to see it, learn to use it and move your audience.

HOW TO CONSTRUCT A STORY USING ARMATURE

As we've examined in our detailed breakdowns of the first acts of *Cast Away* and *Finding Nemo*, it becomes apparent that the armature—the core message or theme—is the driving force that gives meaning and purpose to each narrative choice. These masterfully crafted stories are living proof that an armature is not just an academic concept but an essential tool for the storyteller. So, let's turn our attention to a question that might be on your mind right now: How can you construct your own compelling stories using an armature?

Here we see just how to construct a story when form follows function. The idea of creating a story from an armature seems to baffle many people. I think it's because most have one or several ideas they want to shoehorn into a story. They might know they want a story featuring dragons, for instance. Or perhaps they're captivated by the idea of robots in the Wild West. Sometimes, it's a character that grips them—a young girl growing up on a small farm at the turn of the 20th century.

There is nothing wrong with starting to create a story from ideas such as these, but they are not stories—not yet. The trick, once again, is in finding an armature—a reason to tell a story.

Some storytellers dive into writing, hoping to discover their story's purpose along the way. While this can work, it often results in wasted effort creating scenes, characters, and settings that don't contribute to a cohesive, focused story. Starting with an armature can be challenging, but it often yields stories with stronger momentum and focus. It helps streamline your storytelling, minimizing waste.

A common question is how to use an armature for decision-making, such as character and scene creation. Starting with an idea moves you from the outside in; starting with an armature works from the inside out, guiding your choices. Remember, an effective armature is a provable or disprovable sentence that informs your decisions. For instance, Mark Twain's maxim, "Do the thing you fear most and the death of fear is certain," implies a character plagued by a particular fear.

Examples of this in cinema include *Jaws, Aliens,* and *The King's Speech,* where protagonists must confront their fears. Your armature helps define the types of scenes and characters you'll need. Acts 1 and 3 serve as "before" and "after" pictures, with Act 2 documenting the transformative journey. By the story's climax, the protagonist must face their fear head-on.

If you're struggling to define your armature, consider your protagonist's arc. Knowing how they change and what prompts this change can serve as an implicit armature.

The single most important technique for story construction is the armature. Centering your story around it brings many other elements into alignment.

Now let's examine a cinematic triumph that masterfully utilizes an armature: *Star Trek II: The Wrath of Khan,* widely regarded as the franchise's best installment. I've touched on this film in a previous blog post, but it bears revisiting here to underscore my point.

Star Trek II: The Wrath of Khan breakdown using the armature as a compass

The classic *Star Trek II: The Wrath of Khan* is considered by many to be the best production in the Star Trek film franchise. Let's take a close look at its construction. I have written about this subject before for an old blog post, but I will include it here to help illustrate my point.

As I understand it, *Wrath of Khan*'s story was conceived by producer Harve Bennett, who wrote an outline for the film and then brought on writer Jack B. Sowards to pen the screenplay.

The film's director, Nicholas Meyer, is himself a novelist and no slouch as a writer. (He had already written and directed a film called *Time After Time* about Jack the Ripper escaping into the 20th century using H.G. Wells' time machine, so Wells must track him down.)

When Meyer was brought in, the script needed help, and he rewrote the movie in just 12 days, though he did not take a writing credit. The story served as a kind of sequel to an episode of the original Star Trek television series called "Space Seed," where the crew of the *USS Enterprise* does battle with Khan—a genetically enhanced human being.

Star Trek II starts with what appears to be a dangerous mission: a starship must decide whether to cross into an area called the Neutral Zone to rescue a ship in trouble. However, crossing into this Neutral Zone is an act of war. The person in the captain's chair decides to risk war and attempt a rescue, an act seen as aggression by the enemy (the Klingons), who attack the starship. During the attack, many of the bridge officers are killed, including Mr. Spock.

When all seems lost, a door slides open and a figure enters, calling for the lights to be turned up—this figure is Captain (now-Admiral) Kirk. With his entrance, the "dead" rise and brush themselves off.

As it turns out, this scene is a simulation—a test called the Kobayashi Maru, designed to put young officers in the position of having to make an impossible decision—a "no-win scenario." It's a chance for them to face death.

Dr. McCoy questions staffing the Starship *Enterprise* with inexperienced cadets and mentions it to Kirk as the old bridge crew looks on:

> MCCOY
> Admiral, wouldn't it be easier to put an
> experienced crew back on the ship?
>
> KIRK
> Galloping around the cosmos is a game for
> the young, Doctor.

Kirk Exits

> UHURA
> Now, what is that supposed to mean?

We see that Kirk is unhappy about getting older. This story deals with Kirk facing his own mortality, and through accepting death, he learns to appreciate life.

Soon after the film's opening, Kirk meets up with his old friend Spock. Upon seeing him, Kirk jokes, referring to the simulation, "Aren't you dead?" This is a bit of foreshadowing, as this is a film where Spock does die.

See how the film has just begun, and already the subjects of death and aging have come up so naturally? Not missing a beat, it is in this scene where Spock presents Kirk with a birthday gift—an old book.

> KIRK
> (reading from book)
> "It was the best of times, it was the worst of
> times." —Message, Spock?

> SPOCK
> None that I'm conscious of. Except. of course, happy birthday! —Surely the best of times.

The book is, of course, Dickens' *A Tale of Two Cities*, and its opening line is significant in this story. Kirk does not seem happy about his birthday—for him, this is not the best of times.

Later, Kirk's old friend Dr. McCoy visits Kirk's home with a birthday gift. Along with a bottle of alien spirits, McCoy also brings the gift of reading glasses, again emphasizing the theme of aging.

It's revealed that Kirk is not content being an administrator, feeling his age and adhering to his belief that "galloping around the cosmos is a game for the young."

> MCCOY
> Damn it, Jim, what the hell is the matter with you? Other people have birthdays; why are we treating yours like a funeral?

(He could just as easily have said, "Damn it, Jim, this should be the best of times, and you're treating it as the worst of times!")

These dualities of old and young, life and death, creation and destruction are central to this piece.

Later in the story, Khan, an old enemy of Kirk's, takes over a starship called *The Reliant* to seek revenge on Kirk. Khan discovers something called "Project Genesis," and he finds a way to lure Kirk into a trap using an old love interest, Dr. Carol Marcus, who oversees Project Genesis.

Caught off guard, Kirk is attacked when *The Reliant*, a starship in his fleet, fires on his ship, causing significant damage. At this point, with the *Enterprise* all but dead in space, Khan reveals himself as the attacker. He demands Kirk's surrender and the transfer of all information regarding Project Genesis. Kirk stalls Khan while he "receives" the Genesis data; we see him hesitate as he puts on his eyeglasses—a symbol of the weaknesses of age.

Kirk manages to outsmart Khan, damaging the villain's starship.

Later, Kirk, Spock, and McCoy search their computer for information on the Genesis Project. They learn that it is a kind of missile that can turn a dead moon into a thriving ecosystem. The discussion that follows is this:

> MCCOY
>
> Dear Lord. You think we're intelligent enough to... suppose... what if this thing were used where life already exists?
>
> SPOCK
>
> It would destroy such life in favor of its new matrix.
>
> MCCOY
>
> Its "new matrix"? Do you have any idea what you're saying?
>
> SPOCK
>
> I was not attempting to evaluate its moral implications, Doctor. As a matter of cosmic history, it has always been easier to destroy than to create.
>
> MCCOY
>
> Not anymore; now we can do both at the same time! According to myth, the Earth was created in six days. Now, watch out! Here comes Genesis! We'll do it for you in six minutes!

> SPOCK
>
> Really, Dr. McCoy. You must learn to govern your passions; they will be your undoing. Logic suggests...
>
> MCCOY
>
> Logic? My God, the man's talking about logic; we're talking about universal Armageddon! You green-blooded, inhuman...

From a story construction standpoint, Project Genesis is brilliant—it both creates and destroys life. Again, this duality of life and death intermingles. The best of times, the worst of times.

This theme of life and death, young and old, persists throughout the film. During the story, Kirk meets his son: Birth. And he also loses his best friend: Death.

It's revealed that Kirk cheated when he took the Kobayashi Maru as a cadet. He has never faced death until now.

At the film's climax, Spock gallantly sacrifices his life so that others can live. This teaches Kirk the value of facing death head-on. Both the antagonist, Khan, and Mr. Spock face death in the end. Khan does so by activating the Genesis device onboard his ship, which he believes will not only destroy him but his nemesis Captain Kirk and Kirk's ship, the *Enterprise*. Spock, on the other hand, faces death by sacrificing himself for the good of the crew. This is their Kobayashi Maru. Spock's self-sacrifice makes it clear to Kirk just how precious life is.

Notice how even Spock's death is about the duality of life and death—he dies to save lives.

By the way, in the story of *A Tale of Two Cities*, the protagonist sacrifices his life for someone he loves. This book was not chosen at random.

Near the film's end when Kirk sits down to read the book that Spock had given him for his birthday, he finds that his glasses are broken. He is not an old man. He then has this talk with his son:

> DAVID MARCUS
>
> Lieutenant Slavic was right: You never have faced death.
>
> KIRK
>
> No. Not like this. I haven't faced death. I've cheated death. I've tricked my way out of death and patted myself on the back for my ingenuity. I know nothing.
>
> DAVID MARCUS
>
> You knew enough to tell Saavik that how we face death is at least as important as how we face life.
>
> KIRK
>
> Just words.
>
> DAVID MARCUS
>
> But good words.

Lastly, as Kirk looks out at the newly formed Genesis planet, where they have deposited the body of Spock, he recites some of *A Tale of Two Cities*:

> KIRK
>
> It's a far, far better thing I do than I have ever done before. A far better resting place that I go to than I have ever known.

CAROL MARCUS
Is that a poem?

KIRK
No. Something Spock was trying to tell me.
On my birthday.

MCCOY
You okay, Jim? How do you feel?

KIRK
Young. I feel young.

See how the entire film is constructed around the armature of making peace with death? "How we face death is at least as important as how we face life."

This kind of focus can elevate your stories to a higher level. No matter what the subject or genre might be, you can make your stories stand above the crowd with the application of Invisible Ink.

Star Trek II: The Wrath of Khan is an excellent example of and a great model to follow and to learn from.

The inescapable three-act structure: A lesson from Sherman Alexie

Some argue that the concept of three-act structure is a mere Hollywood construct. Acclaimed Native-American writer Sherman Alexie, for example, doesn't believe in its existence. But regardless of belief or skepticism, three-act structure is nearly inescapable when we share our stories. It's not a manufactured idea but a natural one. We fall into it, often without even realizing what we are doing. To illustrate this, I'm sharing a chapter that first appeared on my Invisible Ink Blog in 2006 and has found its way into various corners of my other works, including my book *Ink Spots*. Though you may have seen it elsewhere, its message and its evidence of three-act structure's inherent place in storytelling are too crucial not to revisit here.

Many years ago, I was invited to speak about storytelling alongside Sherman Alexie at a convention for high school media students. As fate would have it, nobody had informed Sherman about the shared speaking time. He took up the entire slot, but little did I know that his presentation would offer a perfect example of natural story structure.

Sherman Alexie holds the view that formalized story structure—what many call the three-act structure—is a Hollywood fabrication. He opened his talk by dismissing the very idea of a three-act structure and scoffing at the concept of a happy ending. "Life isn't that neat," he claimed.

He then dove into his personal journey, explaining that as a sickly child growing up on a reservation, he had aspired to be a pediatrician. His primary interactions were with medical professionals, so it seemed like a fitting dream. He read all the books in the reservation library and fantasized about his future career. This ideal was put to the test when he enrolled in premed anatomy classes, which required students to dissect cadavers.

On his first day of dissection, the sight of the cadaver caused him to faint. Despite his initial reservations, he was convinced to stay in the class. Later, another fainting episode ensued when the cadaver inadvertently "released gas" during the dissection. Once more, he considered quitting but was talked into staying. However, a third fainting spell finally led him to drop the class for good.

Lost and disoriented about his future, Sherman saw an opening in a poetry class and enrolled. This class introduced him to poetry written by Native Americans, like him, a revelation that had a significant impact on him. Eventually, Sherman had to write a poem for an assignment. The overwhelmingly positive reactions from his female classmates solidified his decision. "That," he said, "is how I became a writer."

What's particularly striking about Sherman's narrative is the irony of its construction. He began by rejecting the notion of a three-act structure and happy endings. However, his own life story, as he shared it, followed a perfect three-act structure and concluded with a personally fulfilling resolution.

So, when we talk about the invisible ink beneath the words, we're really talking about the inescapable rhythms and patterns that guide our storytelling, whether we acknowledge them or not. Sherman Alexie may not believe in a three-act structure, but his own story organically unfolded in just that way, culminating in a satisfying ending. The point here is simple: We may think we're merely writing, but whether we like it or not, we're always telling stories, and more often than not, they fall into structures that are as natural as breathing.

Why a *deus ex machina* doesn't make a satisfying story

For those who are unfamiliar with the term, *deus ex machina* (pronounced DAY-oos EKS MAH-kinna) translates from Latin as "god from the machine." Historically, it refers to a theatrical device where a god would be lowered onto the stage by machinery to solve a play's problems. Nowadays, it signifies a situation where a storyteller pulls a solution out of nowhere, often creating an unsatisfying conclusion.

In ancient Greece, some playwrights used this device to end their plays by having a god descend from Mt. Olympus and resolve everything. This method resulted in the hero not solving the problem himself, and over time, audiences grew weary of this tactic. But why? Aristotle once said, "The resolution of a plot must arise internally, following from the previous action of the play." But why is this the case?

The reason relates to what I said earlier in this book about stories serving as vehicles to transmit survival strategies or information.

Stories act as dress rehearsals for real-life conflicts. Whether set in a fantastical realm or the real world, whether the characters are humans or animals, stories usually provide survival insights. Even if the main character only learns something about themselves or the world, the lesson learned is essential for survival.

Consider the first Indiana Jones film, *Raiders of the Lost Ark*. In his quest to prevent the Biblical Ark of the Covenant from falling into Nazi hands, Indiana Jones initially laughs off the Ark's mystical power. But by the story's climax, he has changed his belief and recognizes something beyond mere historical significance. When the Ark's power is unleashed, killing everyone but him and Marion, it's not the "god from the machine" that saves him but his personal growth and newfound belief.

This situation works in the story because it's not about physical escape but emotional transformation. It illustrates how being open to change can be a lifesaver—a lesson that resonates with many readers.

However, when deus ex machina is used improperly, it feels like a betrayal. The audience is invested in seeing characters overcome their challenges, learn from their experiences, and grow. If a random force or coincidence solves everything, the audience feels cheated.

Conceivably a deus ex machina might work if the story's lesson is centered around hope, belief, or miracles. Still, it must be carefully crafted to teach about emotional or spiritual survival rather than merely extricating characters from a tight spot.

The problem with deus ex machina is that it fails to teach us how to solve problems or survive, making it a clumsy and unsatisfying storytelling tool, akin to visible ink in a world where invisible ink elevates the narrative.

What it means to dramatize an idea

Seeing is different than being told.
—African proverb

I have often had conversations with people who say they like a film or story because it deals with a certain subject, such as sexism or racism. Then, later, when I see the film, I will see that the subject has not been dealt with at all, only spoken about.

Look at this scene from *The Wizard of Oz*, where Dorothy meets the Scarecrow:

THE WIZARD OF OZ
by Noel Langley
Florence Ryerson and Edgar Allan Woolf, 1939

DOROTHY
... you did say something, didn't you?

The Scarecrow shakes his head, then nods — Dorothy looks at the Scarecrow as he nods his head — she speaks to him —

DOROTHY (CONT'D)
Are you doing that on purpose, or can't you
make up your mind?

The Scarecrow explains — shows his straw head.

> SCARECROW
> That's the trouble. I can't make up my mind. I haven't got a brain—only straw.

> DOROTHY
> How can you talk if you haven't got a brain?

> SCARECROW
> I don't know. But some people without brains do an awful lot of talking, don't they?

> DOROTHY
> Yes, I guess you're right.

Dorothy steps over the fence and into the cornfield.

> DOROTHY
> Well, we haven't really met properly, have we?

> SCARECROW
> Why, no.

Dorothy curtsies.

> DOROTHY
> How do you do?

> SCARECROW
> How do you do?

> DOROTHY
> Very well, thank you.

> SCARECROW
> Oh, I'm not feeling at all well. You see, it's very tedious being stuck up here all day long with a pole up your back.

                              DOROTHY

         Oh, dear—that must be terribly

         uncomfortable. Can't you get down?

Dorothy moves around to the back of the pole—

                             SCARECROW

         Down? No, you see, I'm—Well,—I'm—

                              DOROTHY

         Oh, well, here—let me help you.

                             SCARECROW

         Oh, that's very kind of you—very kind.

Dorothy examines the back of the Scarecrow as she tries to unfasten him—

                              DOROTHY

         Well, oh, dear—I don't quite see how I can—

                             SCARECROW

         Of course, I'm not bright about things, but if

         you'll just....

Dorothy follows the Scarecrow's directions—

                             SCARECROW

         ...bend the nail down in the back, maybe I'll

         slip off and...

                              DOROTHY

         Oh....

Dorothy turns the nail, and the Scarecrow falls to the ground.

In this scene the Scarecrow is introduced, and one of the first things he says is that he doesn't have a brain. But it is he who knows how best to get him off his pole, not Dorothy.

Here's another scene:

Dorothy and Scarecrow come forward along Yellow Brick Road. Dorothy reacts as she sees an apple orchard. She goes up to one of the trees.

> DOROTHY
>
> Oh—apples—Oh, look! Oh. Oh—

Dorothy picks an apple off—reacts as the tree takes the apple back and slaps Dorothy's hand—

> DOROTHY
>
> Ouch!

First Tree opens its "mouth" and speaks to Dorothy.

> TREE
>
> What do you think you're doing?
>
> DOROTHY
>
> We've been walking a long ways and I was hungry and—Did you say....

The First Tree gestures as it speaks—

> FIRST TREE
>
> She was hungry! Well, how would you like to have someone come along and pick something off of you?
>
> DOROTHY
>
> Oh, dear—I keep forgetting I'm not in Kansas.

SCARECROW

Come along, Dorothy—you don't want any of those apples. Hmm!

FIRST TREE

What do you mean—she doesn't want any of those apples? Are you hinting my apples aren't what they ought to be?

SCARECROW

Oh, no! It's just that she doesn't like little green....

The Tree reacts, makes a grab for the two—the Scarecrow fights him off as Dorothy runs off, the Scarecrow follows her.

TREE

...you...

SCARECROW

Go—Go!

TREE

...Oh—Help—let me out. I'll give you little green worms.

SCARECROW

I'll show you how to get apples.

TREE (o.s.)

You can't...

The First Tree winds up, throws apples.

> TREE
>
> …do that to me! I'll…

Scarecrow and Dorothy react as the apples begin to hit them. Scarecrow falls back to the road—

> TREE
>
> …show you!

The Trees throw apples at Scarecrow and Dorothy and Toto in the b.g.— The Scarecrow rises, dodges about—

> TREES
>
> You can't do that! You can't do that! Hey!

First Tree laughs as it throws apples.

> SCARECROW
>
> Hooray!

Scarecrow picks up the apples.

> SCARECROW
>
> Hooray! I guess that did it! Help yourself.

There it is again. It is the Scarecrow who has the plan to get the apples, not Dorothy. You may be thinking that this type of writing is too obvious. But how many times have you seen *The Wizard of Oz* and never noticed that the Scarecrow comes up with all of the plans? It was invisible to you—invisible ink.

Here is a great little scene for the Lion, the Tin Man, and the Scarecrow. Remember, the Tin Man thinks he has no heart, and the Lion believes himself a coward.

Tin Man, Lion, and Scarecrow peer over the rocks.

> SCARECROW
>
> That's the castle of the Wicked Witch! Dorothy's in that awful place!
>
> TIN MAN
>
> Oh, I hate to think of her in there. We've got to get her out.

Tin Man cries.

> SCARECROW
>
> Don't cry now. We haven't got the oil-can with us and you've been squeaking enough as it is.
>
> LION
>
> Who's them? Who's them?

The Witch's Winkies are marching about in the Castle Courtyard.

The Lion tries to turn back, but others grab him, push him forward—

> SCARECROW
>
> I've got a plan how to get in there.
>
> LION
>
> Fine. He's got a plan.
>
> SCARECROW
>
> And you're going to lead us.
>
> LION
>
> Yeah. Me?
>
> SCARECROW
>
> Yes, you.

> LION
>
> I—I—I—I—gotta get her outta there?
>
> SCARECROW
>
> That's right.
>
> LION
>
> All right, I'll go in there for Dorothy—Wicked Witch or no Wicked Witch—guards or no guards—I'll tear 'em apart. [growls] I may not come out alive, but I'm going in there. There's only one thing I want you fellows to do.
>
> SCARECROW AND TIN MAN
>
> What's that?
>
> LION
>
> Talk me out of it.

Again, we see that the Scarecrow has a plan, but we also see that the Tin Man has a heart because he tears up. And the Lion gets a chance to show his courage in the face of fear.

By the time we get to the end of *The Wizard of Oz*, we know (at least, subconsciously) that the foursome of the Lion, the Tin Man, the Scarecrow, and Dorothy already have what they've been seeking. We, as an audience, were able to figure it out, and with that comes satisfaction. This happens on almost a subconscious level.

This is what is meant by dramatization. It is showing rather than telling. We know that those things to which we have an emotional connection stick with us better than those for which we have none. Dramatization is a way to get your intellectual ideas across to your audience emotionally.

Do you think anyone watching *Terminator* for the first time thought to themselves: The theme of this film is that none of us knows how important our lives might be? Of course they didn't. What they thought was: RUN! Get the hell away from that thing! But believe me, they got the message of the film, whether they can articulate it or not.

Don't be afraid to entertain—a spoonful of sugar helps the medicine go down.

Jaws is another example of a film that dramatizes, in a very entertaining way, its theme. The character of Chief Brody is terrified of the water. It is something we learn about him early on. At the end of the film, after he has killed the shark, his last line is, "You know, I used to hate the water." He learned that to face his fear was to conquer his fear. The shark was an external representation of Brody's internal fear. If you think that this is something I'm reading into the film, look at the evidence and ask yourself, why would killing a shark rid Brody of his fear of water? It doesn't make any logical sense, but it makes all the sense in the world, thematically.

The following is a story by Aesop.

"Bundle of Sticks"

Once there was a farmer whose many sons were always bickering and fighting with each other. One day the farmer called his sons together. He had with him a bundle of sticks tied together.

He commanded each son to take the bundle and break it in half. In turn they tried and failed. The farmer then untied the bundle, handed each son a single stick and told them to break the sticks now, which they did with ease.

"You see, my sons," said the farmer, "if you are of one mind and unite to assist each other, you will be unaffected by all the attacks of your enemies; but if you are divided among yourselves, you will be broken as easily as these sticks."

Armature (moral): In unity there is strength.

Aesop lived nearly 3,000 years ago, and his stories are still told. Not only are they told, they thrive. They are part of our everyday lives. Everyone knows what we mean when we say someone is a wolf in sheep's clothing. Or if we say someone has sour grapes. Or if we say that someone is crying wolf. All of these sayings are from Aesop's stories.

Why have stories told so long ago stuck around? It is because they had something to say about living as a human being in society, and people haven't changed much since 600 BC. And believe me, as long as there are people, we will have the same problems we have always had.

Aesop's armatures are often called morals, but whatever you call them, it all boils down to the fact that he had a point. Not only that, but he dramatized his point. The farmer in the "Bundle of Sticks" story demonstrates his point to his sons rather than just telling them. This also demonstrates Aesop's point to the reader.

Just as with a joke, these short-form stories have no excess elements. Remember that this is true of any well-crafted story, regardless of length.

I included this story to dramatize the ideas of dramatization and armature.

THEME BEATS LOGIC

Don't give me logic, give me emotion.
—Billy Wilder's instructions to his writing partner, I.A.L. Diamond

Let's start to explore this idea of theme versus logic by looking at the film *Raising Arizona*. Nicolas Cage and Holly Hunter play a couple desperate to have a child. They eventually resort to stealing an infant from a couple with quintuplets.

When the hapless couple bring the baby home, they all pose for a family photo. This snapshot of the new family is followed immediately by a shot of a man's head popping out of a small mud hole. The man screams at the top of his lungs as rain pours down upon him. In the background, we can see a prison wall and searchlight. This man is escaping from prison. Is there any logic at all that says that a man escaping from prison should or would scream as he makes his escape? In fact, logic tells us just the opposite—a man escaping prison would be as quiet as can be. So why is it in the film? It's because theme beats logic, and the mud-soaked screaming man makes a thematic point.

Look where the scene falls in the film—right after the snapshot of the happy family. So what? Think about it: Everything in the scene about the screaming man is made to resemble a birth. The man pops up headfirst. They could have started with his fingers pushing up out of the mud. That would have made logical sense if the man is digging, but this scene is not about logic. The head, covered with dripping mud, emerges from a small hole. The man screams and screams and screams as he is "born" into the world. This is an ugly birth; there is something wrong with this birth. That's the thematic point that beats logic. Nothing good happens for the Nick Cage and Holly Hunter characters after they steal the child. In fact, the escaped convict, along with another, seeks refuge at the couple's home. Hunter and Cage have no choice but to house the criminals because the criminals know about the kidnapping and threaten to expose their secret. The couple has no end of trouble until, at the film's conclusion, they return the child to his rightful parents.

This is a situation in which the armature is not spoken but is evident in every decision made by the storytellers. The armature could be stated as "It is wrong to deprive others of their happiness to gain your own." Or it could be stated as "Nothing good can come from a bad deed."

You may have your own way of putting the film's armature into words; make sure you can back it up with solid, consistent evidence in the story's structure.

Groundhog Day and *Tootsie* have similar armatures: When the protagonists use their inside information to get the object of their desire into bed, it doesn't work. In both cases the plan should work, but it doesn't work because it isn't right thematically.

In *Tootsie* the armature is set up very well. What you see in the first act is that Dustin Hoffman's character is a good actor, and what makes him a good actor is that he can't lie when he's acting. He has to be true to his character. In life he is a liar, particularly to women. Through living the life of a fictional woman who can be nothing but honest, Dustin's male alter ego learns to be honest with women.

One of my favorite examples of armature is the story of *Groundhog Day*. I read somewhere that the studio wanted some kind of explanation as to why Bill Murray's character was reliving the same day over and over again. They wanted a gypsy curse or something along those lines. From what I understand, that explanation was written and then cut because it didn't work. The reason, I think, is that the situation doesn't need a logical explanation. The audience understands why it is happening. It is what is supposed to happen thematically to teach Bill Murray a lesson. When he learns his lesson, the phenomenon stops and we all know why. We understand that "ever since that day" Bill Murray is a better man.

Remember that dramatizing the armature is a way of getting an intellectual idea across emotionally. If you learn to do this, you'll move more people more often and more deeply.

Another favorite example of mine is in the 1968 version of *Planet of the Apes*. Here the armature is that "Man" is a violent and self-destructive creature. This point is hammered home again and again, topped off by the ending, which reveals that humans destroyed their own world.

Near the middle of the film, before the audience knows that the planet is indeed Earth, there is a courtroom scene. You see, the sentient apes of this world have discovered that Taylor (Charlton Heston) can speak. Humans on this world are mute. The courtroom scene takes place following this discovery.

Up to that point, Taylor had been kept in a cage. There is no logical reason to have this scene in a courtroom. Why not have the scene at Taylor's cage? It all goes back to the armature that Man is a violent and self-destructive creature. This scene, thematically, is about putting humanity on trial. The storytellers even make a point of stripping Taylor of his clothes to make him appear more Adam-like. And it is no mistake that this scene immediately follows the discovery that Taylor possesses speech. Just being human, it seems, is a crime. It is a beautifully crafted scene that abandons logic for theme to support its armature.

THE USE OF CLONES

"Once upon a time there were three little pigs..."

Years ago, a friend of mine, an illustrator, was hired at a studio. There he met one of the best illustrators he'd ever seen. This illustrator had been at the studio for ten years, and he was tired and worn out. The job had been so stressful that it had sapped him of vitality and enthusiasm.

My friend looked at this illustrator and said to himself, "I can't be here for ten years."

He had met a clone character. This is something we all do every day. Just as my friend did, we use the people we meet and know to measure ourselves. We all know people who we think are smarter than us, richer than us, or have a better relationship than us, or any number of things. We can also think the opposite of these things, though we hesitate to admit this in polite company.

What I am calling clones have been called other names—mirror characters and reflection characters—but, whatever you call them, they are useful tools of the storyteller's craft.

A clone in story terms is a tool for showing, not telling. Clones are characters in your story that represent what could, should, or might happen to the protagonist if he or she takes a particular path. Two of the Three Little Pigs are clones. It is the failure of the first two pigs that allows us to measure the success of the last pig. This is a simple use of clones, and one of the most obvious to see.

But clones exist in more complicated stories as well. In J.R.R. Tolkien's *The Lord of the Rings*, the pitiful character of Gollum is used to show what might happen to the hero Frodo if he is seduced by the power of a magic ring. Just as in the story of the three pigs, we measure the success of one character by the failure of another.

In *Tootsie*, the woman who is the object of Dustin Hoffman's desire is dating a lying womanizer. In one scene, Dustin, as a woman, confronts the womanizer and tells him that he understands his womanizing ways better than he thinks. This is a way for Dustin to "see" and confront himself.

Going back to *The Wizard of Oz*, all three of Dorothy's companions are clones. They, like she, are looking for something they already have. Having clones is a way of dramatizing ideas—again, a way of showing instead of telling. As I said earlier, the audience sees that Scarecrow has brains from the very first scene and this is reinforced throughout the story. Perhaps you remember the line, "Don't cry, you'll rust again," said to the Tin Man. Hmm, turns out he does have a heart, after all.

John Steinbeck uses a cast of clones in his novel *Of Mice and Men*. The armature of that story is that people need companionship. It is dramatized as well as stated. If it has been a while since you've read it, I suggest you reread it soon. It is amazingly well-crafted. Steinbeck knows what he wants to say and says it over and over again in different ways. And he does give you an intellectual idea on an emotional level.

In the story, George and Lennie are two migrant workers who travel and work together. Lennie, being mentally challenged, is a lot of trouble for George, but George's need for companionship and his love for Lennie make the relationship worth the trouble. Other characters even comment on how strange it is for these two to travel together.

One of the first things to happen is that George discovers that Lennie is petting a dead mouse he is keeping in his pocket. Lennie is a huge man who has no sense of his own strength and had killed the mouse by accident. Lennie enjoys the companionship of small, soft animals, and is obsessed with one day having rabbits to take care of.

When the duo reaches the ranch where they are to work, one of the people they meet is the boss's wife. She often flirts with the ranch hands because her husband doesn't pay attention to her—she craves companionship.

On this ranch there is also an old man who has on old dog. The other hands in the bunkhouse think the dog is worthless. A man named Carlson suggests that the old man shoot the stinky old dog because it has, as he puts it, "Got no teeth. He's all stiff with rheumatism. He ain't no good to you."

The scene goes on with Candy, the old man, protesting, but Carlson won't let go of his idea that the dog should be shot:

> Candy looked about unhappily. "No," he said softly. "No, I couldn't do that. I had 'im too long."
>
> "He don't have no fun," Carlson insisted. "And he stinks to beat hell. Tell you what. I'll shoot him for you. Then it won't be you what does it."
>
> Candy threw his legs off his bunk. He scratched the white stubble whiskers on his cheek nervously. "I'm so used to him," he said softly. "I had him from a pup."
>
> "Well, you ain't bein' kind to him keepin' him alive," said Carlson. "Look, Slim's bitch got a litter right now. I bet Slim would give you one of them pups to raise up, wouldn't you, Slim?"
>
> The skinner had been studying the old dog with his calm eyes. "Yeah," he said. "You can have a pup if you want to." He seemed to shake himself free for speech. "Carl's right, Candy. That dog ain't no good to himself. I wisht somebody'd shoot me if I get old an' a cripple."
>
> Candy looked helplessly at him, for Slim's opinions were law. "Maybe it'd hurt him," he suggested. "I don't mind takin' care of him."

Carlson said: "The way I'd shoot him, he wouldn't feel nothing. I'd put the gun right there." He pointed with his toe. "Right back of the head. He wouldn't even quiver."

At last Carlson said: "If you want me to, I'll put the old devil out of his misery right now and get it over with. Ain't nothing left for him. Can't eat, can't see, can't even walk without hurtin'."

Candy said hopefully: "You ain't got no gun."

"The hell I ain't. Got a Luger. It won't hurt him none at all."

Candy said: "Maybe tomorra. Le's wait till tomorra."

"I don't see no reason for it," said Carlson. He went to his bunk, pulled his bag from underneath it, and took out a Luger pistol. "Let's get it over with," he said. "We can't sleep with him stinkin' around in here." He put the pistol in his hip pocket.

Candy looked a long time at Slim to try to find some reversal. And Slim gave him none. At last Candy said softly and hopelessly: "Awright—take 'im." He did not look down at the dog at all. He lay back on his bunk and crossed his arms behind his head and stared at the ceiling.

From his pocket Carlson took a little leather thong. He stooped over and tied it around the dog's neck. All the men except Candy watched him.

> "Come, boy. Come on, boy," he said gently. And he said apologetically to Candy: "He won't even feel it." Candy did not move nor answer him. He twitched the thong.
> "Come on, boy." The old dog got slowly and stiffly to his feet and followed the gently-pulling leash.
> Carlson takes the dog out to shoot him, and the old man lies on his back looking at the ceiling, and after an agonizingly long time, a shot is heard in the distance. With this, Candy rolls over in his bunk and faces the wall.

We see how much this stinky, old dog means to this man. The dog and the old man are clones of Lennie and George.

How do I know that I'm not reading all of this into the story? One way to know is the repetition of the armature. It is dramatized over and over again. The scene where they shoot the old man's dog is a well- written scene, but what makes it great is that it nails home the armature, using emotion to do so.

Another way the point is nailed home is in the scene wherein George has gone to town with some of the other ranch hands, leaving Lennie alone. Lennie stumbles on Crooks, the black stable hand, in his shed next to the barn. Crooks is not allowed in the bunkhouse because he is black, and as a result is lonesome. During their exchange, Crooks says this to Lennie:

> Crooks said gently: "Maybe you can see now. You got George. You know he's goin' to come back. S'pose you didn't have nobody. S'pose you couldn't go into the bunk-house and play rummy 'cause you was black. How'd you

like that? S'pose you had to sit out here an' read books. Sure you could play horseshoes till it got dark, but then you got to read books. Books ain't no good. A guy needs somebody—to be near him." He whined: "A guy goes nuts if he ain't got nobody. Don't make no difference who the guy is, long's he's with you. I tell ya," he cried, "I tell ya a guy gets too lonely an' he gets sick."

As you can see, the armature is stated. I read or see stories all the time in which characters say wise things and the audience nods knowingly, but it means nothing if the structural elements of the story don't back it up. Every decision one makes when constructing a story must contribute in some way to the armature, or why is it there? Steinbeck makes good use of clones in this story. And if you doubt for a minute the old man's dog isn't a clone for Lennie, at one point Crooks speculates about Lennie without George: "Want me ta tell ya what'll happen? They'll take ya to the booby hatch. They'll tie ya up with a collar, like a dog."

Steinbeck was a master at the use of invisible ink. He understood how secondary characters could help solidify his armature and dramatize his point. One of the ironies of invisible ink is just how blatant one can be when applying it. The audience will never see it unless they have been trained to see the footprints in the grass.

The aforementioned *Finding Nemo* makes excellent use of clones that help to illustrate the film]s point.

Marlin's companion as he searches for his son is a forgetful and eternally optimistic fish named Dory. Dory is a clone for Marlin. Marlin is plagued by memory, making him uptight and anxious, while Dory, who has no memory, is easygoing and cheerful. When we have Dory to compare to Marlin, it shows us another way that Marlin could operate in the world.

Another clone for Marlin is a laid-back sea turtle named Crush, whom he meets later in the film. Crush parents in the exact opposite way from Marlin. The turtle allows his children to test their limits, explore, and get themselves out of potential dangers. Now we can compare the parenting styles and see another way that Marlin could behave.

Nemo has been captured and put into a fish tank with a group of tropical fish. That tank has a de facto leader named Gill. Gill is the father figure of the tank. Gill is a brilliant clone character because he is both a clone for Marlin and for Nemo.

He is a father figure who allows Nemo to take risks. Being a father figure, he is, of course, a clone for Marlin. However, he also has a damaged fin, mirroring Nemo's disability – his "lucky fin." He shows us, and Nemo, what Nemo could accomplish given the chance. This is an absolutely brilliant use of a clone.

Another example from Pixar is their very first film, *Toy Story*. Woody, the cowboy toy, is the favorite toy of a boy named Andy. Woody's world is shaken by the addition of a new toy, a high-tech adventuring astronaut toy called Buzz Lightyear.

Andy pays more attention to Buzz and less to Woody. Woody feels discarded and unloved.

Buzz is a clone for Woody. Woody watches as Buzz takes his position.

But there is a clone for Andy that helps Woody see the situation differently.

While Andy is a kind and loving boy who treats his toys well, the neighbor, Sid, is a sadistic kid who tortures his toys. When Buzz and Woody find themselves trapped at Sid's house, they see just how bad life could be. Woody sees that Andy has enough love to go around.

In the sequel, *Toy Story 2*, Woody meets a clone, Jessie, a cowgirl toy who has been discarded when the little girl who owned her gets too old to play with dolls.

Woody becomes concerned that Andy will grow out of wanting to play with toys. He becomes afraid that he too will be abandoned.

Like my friend comparing himself to the older illustrator, Woody sees his possible future.

Jessie's pain allows us to feel Woody's feelings. We know why he is afraid.

Can clones be used in more adult stories? Of course. A great example is the film *The Shawshank Redemption*.

The 1994 film was adapted by Frank Darabont from the Stephen King book *Rita Hayworth and Shawshank Redemption*. The armature of the piece is: "Get busy living, or get busy dying." The story takes place in a prison and centers on a character named Andy Dufresne, played by actor Tim Robbins. Dufresne exemplifies the armature by refusing to succumb to the darkness of the prison. He has an almost supernatural ability to remain optimistic despite the harsh circumstances of Shawshank State Penitentiary. This is Andy Dufresne getting busy living rather than getting busy dying.

In the story, an older inmate, called Brooks, is released after a long sentence. He finds the world outside of prison impossible to bear. His long years behind bars have caused him to become "institutionalized," as explained by another long-time inmate called Red, played by Morgan Freeman.

Red explains becoming institutionalized in this way: "These walls are funny. First you hate 'em, then you get used to 'em. Enough time passes, you get so you depend on them. That's institutionalized.... The man's been in here fifty years, Heywood. Fifty years! This is all he knows. In here, he's an important man. He's an educated man. Outside, he's nothing! Just a used-up con with arthritis in both hands."

As you will see, Brooks and Red are clones.

Brooks gets an apartment and a job, which he hates, as a "bag boy" at the grocery store. He is thrown by the quick pace of life since he was put away.

His narration, a letter to his friends back at Shawshank, tells us how he's feeling:

> "Dear Fellas, I can't believe how fast things move on the outside. I saw an automobile once when I was a kid, but now they're everywhere. The world went and got itself in a big damn hurry."

With his next actions, Brooks demonstrates what it means to get busy dying. His letter continues:

> "...I don't think the store manager likes me very much. Sometimes after work I go to the park and feed the birds. I keep thinking Jake might just show up and say hello. But he never does. I hope wherever he is, he's doing okay and making new friends. I have trouble sleeping at night. I have—bad dreams, like I'm falling. I wake up scared. Sometimes it takes me a while to remember where I am. Maybe I should get me a gun and rob the Food-Way, so they'd send me home. I could shoot the manager while I was at it, sort of like a bonus."

Brooks puts on a suit and tie, stands on a chair, and carves into a beam in his apartment: "Brooks was here."

> "I guess I'm too old for that sort of nonsense anymore. I don't like it here. I'm tired of being afraid all the time. I've decided not to stay. I doubt they'll kick up any fuss. Not for an old crook like me."

Brooks then hangs himself. He has gotten busy dying. At that point, he is a clone for Andy Dufresne. The contrast between Dufresne and Brooks is clear; one gets busy living while the other gets busy dying.

Later, when Red is released from Shawshank, he finds himself in exactly the same situation as Brooks before him. He has the same job at the grocery store, lives in the same apartment, and even sleeps under the carved message from Brooks.

The stark contrast between Red and Brooks—both clones for Andy—is evident when Red, also feeling the weight of the world outside, stands on the chair, carving into the beam next to Brooks's name: "So was Red."

But instead of giving in to despair, Red reflects on his promise to Andy, eventually finding the courage to pursue a new life. He gets busy living.

Clone characters are integral to storytelling, illuminating different facets of the main characters and the themes of the story. They enable us to feel the struggles and triumphs of the characters more deeply, making the experience richer and more engaging. Whether it's Andy Dufresne in *The Shawshank Redemption* or Woody in *Toy Story*, clones give a profound understanding of the characters' motives and choices, and they lead us to question what we would do in their place.

Another master of invisible ink was storyteller Paddy Chayefsky. He used clones with deft skill in his teleplay and movie *Marty*.

Marty was a television play written in the 1950s. It made such a huge impact that the network was deluged with letters asking that it be performed again. This was in the days of live television, and there were no such things as reruns. Not only was it performed again, but it was made into a film that won the Best Picture Oscar™.

Marty is about an Italian American man who can't seem to get a date. He is considered ugly, and in his world he is also considered the male equivalent of an old maid. He lives with his mother, who pesters him to get married. These elements are the conflict in the piece. So, at the fulcrum of the story, Marty finds a woman who likes him. Problem solved. This is what both Marty and his mother have wanted. But here's the thing about drama: lack of conflict kills it. So where does the conflict come in now? Marty's mother has a clone, her sister. So what Chayefsky does now is brilliant. After Marty meets his girlfriend, and it looks like things are going well, Chayefsky cuts to this scene:

Then the mother addresses herself to Aunt Catherine.

MOTHER:
We gotta postcard from my son, Nickie, and his bride this morning. They're in Florida inna big hotel. Everything is very nice.

AUNT
That's nice.

MOTHER
Catherine, I want you come live with me in my house with Marty and me. In my house, you have your own room. You don't have to sleep onna couch inna living room like here.

The aunt looks slowly and directly at the mother.

> MOTHER (CONT'D)

Catherine, your son is married. He got his own home. Leave him in peace. He wants to be alone with his wife. They don't want no old lady sitting inna balcony. Come and live with me. We will cook in the kitchen and talk like when we were girls. You are dear to me, and you are dear to Marty. We are pleased for you to come.

> AUNT

Did they come to see you?

> MOTHER

Yes.

> AUNT

Did my son Thomas come with her?

> MOTHER

Your son Thomas was there.

> AUNT

Did he also say he wishes to cast his mother from his house?

> MOTHER

Catherine, don't make an opera outta this. The three-a you anna baby live in three skinny rooms. You are an old goat, and she has an Italian temper. She is a good girl, but you drive her crazy. Leave them alone. They have their own life.

The old aunt turns her head slowly and looks her sister square in the face. Then she rises slowly from her chair.

> AUNT
> (Coldly)
> Get outta here. This is my son's house. This is where I live. I am not to be cast out inna street like a newspaper.

The mother likewise rises. The two old women face each other directly.

> MOTHER
> Catherine, you are very dear to me. We have cried many times together. When my husband died, I would have gone insane if it were not for you. I ask you to come to my house because I can make you happy. Please come to my house.

The two sisters regard each other. Then Aunt Catherine sits again in her oaken chair, and the mother returns to her seat. The hardened muscles in the old aunt's face suddenly slacken, and she turns to her sister.

> AUNT
> Theresa, what shall become of me?

> MOTHER
> Catherine.

> AUNT
> It's gonna happen to you. Mark it well. These terrible years. I'm afraida look inna mirror. I'm afraid I'm gonna see an old lady with white hair, like the old ladies inna park, little bundles inna black shawl, waiting for the coffin. I'm fifty-six years old. What am I to do with

myself? I have strength in my hands. I wanna cook. I wanna clean. I wanna make dinner for my children. I wanna be of use to somebody. Am I an old dog to lie in fronta the fire till my eyes close. These are terrible years, Theresa. Terrible years!

MOTHER

Catherine, my sister…

The old aunt stares, distraught, at the mother.

AUNT

It's gonna happen to you! It's gonna happen to you! What will you do if Marty gets married! What will you cook?! What happen to alla children tumbling in alla rooms?! Where is the noise?! It is a curse to be a widow. A curse! What will you do if Marty gets married?! What will you do?!

She stares at the mother—her deep, gaunt eyes haggard and pained. The mother stares back for a moment, then her own eyes close. The aunt has hit home. The aunt sinks back onto her chair, sitting stiffly, her arms on the thick armrests. The mother sits hunched a little forward, her hands nervously folded in her lap.

AUNT

(Quietly)

I will put my clothes inna bag and I will come to you tomorrow.

[The camera slowly dollies back from the two somber sisters.]

SLOW FADE-OUT.

This starts to worry Marty's mother and she changes her attitude about his getting married. It's very skillfully done and keeps the conflict, and therefore the interest, going.

Understand that not all stories use clones, but they are useful tools to put in your storyteller's toolbox. A storyteller should know why every character in their story exists. They should not be there just to "flesh out the world," as I often hear my students say.

In Alfred Hitchcock's *Rear Window*, Jimmy Stewart plays a man with a broken leg who doesn't want to marry his girlfriend, Grace Kelly. Jimmy plays a photojournalist who lives a life of high adventure. In fact, he broke his leg while shooting a race car accident. The reason he doesn't want to marry his fashion designer girlfriend is that he feels she doesn't have enough backbone. He feels they would be incompatible in a happily-ever-after situation.

Jimmy is confined to a wheelchair and so he passes the time by looking out his window and spying on his neighbors. The thing is, all of the neighbors are clones. They are all in various stages of romantic relationships. There is a honeymoon couple, an older childless couple, a sexy woman who has men fawning over her, a woman who can't get a date, and a couple that is always arguing—each one a distorted clone of Jimmy and Grace.

By the way, Jimmy changes his mind about Grace when he believes that one of his neighbors has murdered his wife and he sees just how much backbone she has as she throws herself into the adventure.

To the untrained eye, clone characters appear to be nothing more than secondary characters populating the story's world. But in the hands of a skillful storyteller, they are the invisible ink that helps illuminate the story's point.

CHAPTER IV

Charged Objects

- What is a charged object?
- Ritual pain
- The power of sacrifice in stories
- From butterfly to caterpillar
- Killing the protagonist

> *"Objects have stories; stories have objects.*
> *They entangle themselves."*
>
> — *Tim Ingold, British Anthropologist*

WHAT IS A CHARGED OBJECT?

Psychics use the term "charged objects" for items from a crime scene. These objects might hold residual energy that could provide the psychic with information about the crime.

In storytelling, a "charged object" can be anything that is charged with emotion.

Charged objects, like every other storymaking tool, work because they reflect how things function in the natural world. For instance, imagine your home was burning and you could only save one or two objects. Chances are you would save charged objects like family photos or other things that holds emotional value. These are emotionally charged objects.

Cookie Monster

When I was about seven years old, my favorite character from the popular children's television show *Sesame Street* was the Cookie Monster. I received a much-cherished gift from my mother—a Cookie Monster puppet—which I took everywhere. My mother warned me that I would lose it, but I was sure that I wouldn't. Predictably, I did lose it one evening when I left it at a pizza restaurant. I was crushed.

For years—for decades—whenever I went by that pizza place, I would be reminded of my puppet. Even when the building no longer housed the restaurant but became a liquor store and then a mattress store, I felt a tinge of sadness whenever I passed it.

When I turned fifty years old, my mother presented me with a new Cookie Monster toy. As you might imagine, this toy is a highly charged object.

Anything, any place, or any person can be charged. Have you ever revisited a school you used to attend or passed through an old neighborhood that evoked memories and emotions? A charged place might be the former home of a cherished loved one.

A person one hasn't seen for a very long time might be charged when they reappear in your life.

By the way, anything can be positively or negatively charged. One might have negative feelings about any of these objects, people, or places. The building where I lost my beloved Cookie Monster puppet was negatively charged for years. Now it is positively charged because it is linked to my mother's gesture.

The use of charged objects in storytelling can evoke emotions in one's audience while remaining almost invisible to them when the technique is applied skillfully. The storyteller imbues the object with emotion so that whenever a character interacts with the object, it evokes an emotional reaction in the audience.

Cast Away

Chuck Noland's watch in *Cast Away* is a charged object. And, if you know the film, so is a volleyball called Wilson. If you have any doubt about the power of a charged object, know that the prop volleyball from the film sold at an auction in 2022 for $85,239. That's a lot of money for a volleyball that, at the time of this writing, sells for about $20.

Searching for Bobby Fischer

The excellent 1993 film *Searching for Bobby Fischer* makes powerful use of a piece of paper. This object also ties perfectly into the story's armature, as any good charged object should.

Searching for Bobby Fischer is based on the true story of seven-year-old Josh Waitzkin, who becomes intrigued with chess after watching men play speed chess in the park. When he plays the game with a man at the park, his skill is noticed by the other men. It turns out that Josh is a chess prodigy, drawing comparisons to the legendary Bobby Fischer.

A chess hustler from the park named Vinnie takes an interest in Josh's chess education and teaches him about the game.

At one point in the film, Josh is concerned about Vinnie, wondering if he is homeless and sleeps in the park or has a home. He asks his mother if Vinnie can stay with them.

His mother does not say no to her son's request and is obviously touched by his compassion. She lovingly responds, "You have a good heart; that's what's important."

Josh's struggle in the story is to keep his good heart, and his mother becomes the protector of that heart.

Wanting Josh to get proper instruction, his parents enlist the services of a professional chess instructor named Pandolfini, whose lessons, much to Pandolfini's dismay, differ greatly from Vinnie's instructions.

Pandolfini requests that the parents forbid Josh from playing speed chess in the park because Josh is picking up bad habits, making Pandolfini's job of teaching harder.

Bonnie, the mother and protector of Josh's good heart, refuses to forbid Josh from playing chess with the men in the park because he enjoys it so much. She wants her son to have fun more than she wants him to win competitions.

During one of Josh's lessons, Pandolfini becomes impressed by the young boy's playing ability. Carefully, with a sense of ceremony, Pandolfini extracts a certificate from his briefcase. He is careful not to crease or damage the piece of paper as he presents it to Josh. It's a secret, precious item, and at this moment, it's imbued with great value, becoming a charged object in the context of the story.

The certificate undergoes a transformation later in the film. Pandolfini, disappointed by Josh's obsession with the document, carelessly pulls out one certificate after another. In sharp contrast with the reverence he showed before, he piles them on the table, dismissing them as meaningless garbage. Josh's face crumples, and he is on the brink of tears until his mother, the protector of his heart, intervenes. Suddenly, the once-valuable certificate has lost its worth and is negatively charged.

Later Pandolfini, filled with pride for Josh and his good character as much as his chess acumen, once again presents Josh with the certificate. The gesture transforms the object again, and the certificate becomes positively charged, its value restored and indeed enhanced. It now symbolizes much more than mere achievement; it stands for the very essence of Josh's character.

In *Searching for Bobby Fischer*, this piece of paper undergoes a full arc, moving from valuable to worthless and finally to priceless. This transformation serves as a poignant metaphor in the story, resonating with the audience's own emotional connections to objects in their lives. It is a masterful example of a charged object, displaying its power to evoke emotions in a way that is almost invisible to the audience when applied with skill.

Seabiscuit

In the film *Seabiscuit*, written and directed by Gary Ross based on the best-selling book *Seabiscuit: An American Legend* by Laura Hillenbrand, a charged object gives the audience insight into a character's inner world.

The protagonist, Charles S. Ballard, has a young son who is often seen playing a small hand-held video game. When the boy is killed in a car accident, he has the game with him. For the rest of the film, whenever Ballard is seen holding the game, the audience knows what he is thinking about. This evokes an emotional response in the audience because it triggers our memory and empathy.

It's a Wonderful Life

The classic American film *It's a Wonderful Life* is known for evoking emotions, in no small part due to the use of charged objects. The film is a master class in the application of invisible ink.

George Bailey, the film's protagonist, spends his entire childhood wanting to leave his small hometown of Bedford Falls, travel the world, and plan and build modern cities, but circumstances keep holding him back. He believes that he is stuck, but he is not—he chooses to stay.

It's a Wonderful Life is particularly rich in charged objects, where everything from train whistles to brochures to flower petals represents various states of George Bailey's emotional life. These objects become emotionally charged because of the way the characters interact with them, changing their meaning over the course of the story.

Anchor Chains, Planes, and Train Whistles

In George's life, specific sounds hold significant meaning, serving as powerful symbols that evolve with his experiences and aspirations. These auditory elements—the sounds of anchor chains, planes, and train whistles—encapsulate his complex journey. Initially, they resound with the promise of ambition and dreams, echoing his yearning for adventure. However, as time unfolds, these once-optimistic sounds transform into poignant reminders of disappointment and lost opportunities. Gradually, they become emotionally charged symbols of George's continually deferred dreams, encapsulating the essence of his narrative.

Travel Brochures

Symbolizing George's aspirations, his travel brochures later become negatively charged as he discards them in acceptance of another lost dream.

Zuzu's Flower Petals

These petals that had fallen from the flower of George's young daughter symbolize George's love for his family and his role as a caretaker, reminding him of what truly matters during his moment of despair.

The Building and Loan Company

This entity represents responsibility, community, and George's personal sacrifices for the greater good.

Negatively Charged Objects

The film cleverly shifts the emotional charge of objects, showing George's inner turmoil without explicitly stating it.

Frank Capra, the director, uses these charged objects to deepen our understanding of George Bailey's character. They're more than mere props; they're integral to the narrative, symbolizing George's desires, disappointments, responsibilities, and ultimately his realization of what truly matters.

This film is awash with charged objects, and I challenge you to look for yourself to see what you find.

Charged objects are a powerful tool that can be indispensable in applying invisible ink to your stories. If you learn to use them well, you will be rewarded by the emotional engagement of your audience.

Exercise: Identifying Your Own Charged Objects

In storytelling and in life, a charged object is any person, place, or thing that carries emotional or psychological significance. Whether it's a childhood home, a cherished book, or even a person in your life, these objects are imbued with memories, hopes, or fears, making them more than just their physical form. They become a mirror reflecting our inner world, revealing complexities that might not be immediately apparent. Recognizing these charged objects enriches not only your personal narrative but also the stories you tell.

Objective:

To cultivate a deeper awareness of the emotional significance carried by various objects in your life and in the lives of those around you. This exercise aims not only to help you identify charged objects but also to get into the habit of recognizing them.

Instructions:

1. *Brainstorm a List:* Begin by jotting down objects that hold emotional value to you. Don't rush; your list can grow over days, weeks, or even years.
2. *Categorize the Charge:* Next to each object, note whether its emotional charge is positive, negative, or mixed. Keep in mind that the object's status can change over time.
3. *Tell the Story:* Select a few objects from your list at a time and write a brief explanation of why each holds emotional value for you. Identify the events or experiences that "charged" these objects with emotional weight.
4. *Switch Perspectives:* Imagine these objects appearing in a story. How could they serve to deepen a character's emotional complexity?
5. *Ongoing Practice:* Make a habit of noticing new charged objects in your life and in the lives of those around you. Add them to your list and explore their stories when you have time.

Recognizing charged objects in your storytelling is like using invisible ink that becomes indelible over time. While they may initially seem subtle, these emotionally charged elements etch themselves into the hearts of your audience, turning simple narratives into deeply resonant experiences. By including this practice in your storytelling toolkit, you enrich your work with a layer of emotional truth that remains impactful long after the story has ended.

RITUAL PAIN

Everybody wants to go to heaven, but nobody wants to die.
—*Blues song lyric by D. Nix*

Up to this point I have mentioned character change without discussing the topic in depth. I will get to it in a few seconds.

A few years ago, when I was working on a spec screenplay that involved gangs, I visited a school with a lot of gang activity and asked the kids to tell me how gangs worked. One of the things I found out was that in order to join a gang you had to be "jumped" in. What that means is that you let the other gang members beat the crap out of you for a prescribed amount of time, anywhere from two to five minutes. After that, you are a member of the gang.

This sounded so barbaric to me. I didn't understand why anyone would allow himself or herself to be abused in this way.

A couple of years after that, I was writing a comic book that had an Australian Aborigine as one of the main characters. While doing research, I read about one tribe that would knock one or two teeth out of adolescents as part of their initiation into adulthood.

I thought back to my reaction years earlier when a good friend of mine was rushing a fraternity. I never could have let myself be humiliated the way he allowed himself to be.

I began to see a pattern—groups of men or boys all have some kind of harsh initiation into their fold. It doesn't seem to be anything that has to be taught; it appears to be inherent behavior.

Later, I was talking with an African shaman who lived in my neighborhood, and he began to describe the manhood ceremony in his village. He talked about tribal peoples all over the world having similar ceremonies that involved what he called "ritual pain." Sometimes it is ritual scarification or tattooing. Sometimes it is a solo hunt for a beast. Other times it is a quest to survive alone in the forest. In some cultures it involves circumcision. Blood or the possibility of bloodletting is almost always part of the ritual. Like the street gangs say, "Blood in, blood out," meaning that you must undergo the pain to get into, or get out of, a gang.

In all cases, the purpose of this ritual seems to be about tearing the individual down and then transforming him from boyhood to manhood. At the end of the ritual, he has become a full-fledged member of the group with the rights, privileges, and responsibilities of an adult member of said group.

I asked the shaman about women, and he speculated that women didn't usually have these kinds of ceremonies because they have a natural bloodletting that signifies their transformation from girls to women. Plus, they often have blood and/or pain when they lose their virginity. And we all know that there is pain in childbirth, and that certainly does change a woman. There is female circumcision, but it is imposed by the expectations of men and therefore not included here.

I started to think of this idea in story terms. The second act is a kind of ritual pain that changes your character. Usually your character possesses what has been called a fatal flaw. There is something they need to learn before they can be transformed into a better, more mature person.

What is it that Elliott's brother says to him in E.T.? "Why don't you grow up and think how other people feel?"

We are all resistant to change. There is an old blues song that contains the lyric, "Everybody wants to go to heaven, but nobody wants to die."

More than likely, there is something about yourself that you would like to change or that you should change, but it seems too difficult to do it. I don't know why the world works this way, but the things we should do are always the most difficult, so we rarely run toward change. This is true of your characters as well.

Toy Story and Toy Story 2

In *Toy Story*, Buzz Lightyear refuses to believe that he is a toy and not a space ranger. Also in *Toy Story*, Woody has to learn to share the affection of his owner with Buzz. When you see the film again, you'll notice that this transformation is not easy for them, but they become better "people" when they do change.

In *Toy Story 2*, Woody is in danger of being discarded and meets Jessie, a clone who tells him what his fate might be. It is painful for both of them, but they each realize that they have value.

Understanding the dynamics of story allowed Pixar to make one of the few sequels that measures up to the original. John Lasseter and the people at Pixar understand story as well as anyone. Study these films.

James Cameron's films

Look at *Jaws* again. Take a man afraid of the water, subject him to the ritual pain of doing battle with a shark, and watch as the pain transforms him… cures him.

James Cameron took what could have been a little B-movie and made *Terminator* into a surprise box office hit. He put Linda Hamilton's character, Sarah Connor, through the ritual pain of being hunted down and nearly killed. In the end she is transformed into a woman who knows that her life matters. She has also been hardened by the experience and seems less girlish. She has grown up.

In *Terminator 2: Judgment Day*, Sarah Connor becomes the terminator. It is she who tries to kill a man for something he will do in the future. Through ritual pain she realizes that she has become the very thing she hates.

In *Aliens*, Sigourney Weaver's character, Ripley, is plagued by nightmares of the creature she had survived in the first film in the *Alien* series. Through the ritual pain of battling these creatures again, she purges herself of the nightmares and takes back her life.

Billy Wilder's films

Billy Wilder understood the power of character change so well that when the American Film Institute listed the top one hundred films of all time, four were his.

In *Sunset Boulevard*, Wilder had character Joe Gillis, an out-of-work Hollywood screenwriter, sell out for a little security and become the kept man of an older ex-movie star. He becomes her pet. In fact, when they first meet, the pet chimp of the has-been star has just died. It is no mistake that following this loss, Joe Gillis moves into the woman's home. At one point in the film she dresses Joe in a tux—sometimes called a monkey suit. Through the ritual pain of being a kept man Joe Gillis learns that having a swimming pool isn't worth selling out his principles.

This idea of selling out shows up again and again in other Wilder films. In *The Apartment*, Jack Lemmon plays a man who, to climb the corporate ladder, lends his apartment to adulterous executives at the insurance company where he works. Sometimes this means not getting into his own apartment and having to sleep in the park. He, of course, learns to stand up for himself.

Also in *The Apartment*, Shirley MacLaine plays a woman who is having an affair with one of the aforementioned executives. This idea of selling out, or prostituting oneself, hits hard when the executive, not having time to buy a Christmas present for his mistress, hands Shirley a hundred-dollar bill as a gift. It is through the ritual pain of being made to feel cheap that Shirley learns to respect herself enough to be with a man who will commit to her fully.

The Apartment has two characters who change, but they both learn essentially the same lesson. They are clones of one another.

Because change is never easy, and is resisted, it is your job as storyteller to apply as much pressure on your characters as possible. You must back them into a corner and force them to change. Make it as painful as you can. Bring them to the brink of physical or emotional death if you possibly can. Your protagonists will be measured by the size of their struggle, so don't pull any punches.

Transformative lessons

Those who believe in reincarnation believe that we die and are reborn again and again until we learn whatever we were sent to learn in life. When we finally attain wisdom, we ascend to a higher plane of existence. We are rewarded.

You don't need to believe in reincarnation to see this idea played out. Many of us know people who repeat the same mistakes over and over again throughout their lives. They might, for instance, keep dating people who disrespect them. Until they realize that they are bringing this unhappiness on themselves, they will never be happy. They will never get their reward.

Groundhog Day is a great example of this concept in story form. Bill Murray is, in a sense, reborn every day. At one point he even tries to kill himself to get out of this cycle, but it doesn't work. It is only when he starts to focus on things outside of himself and becomes a better person that he is able to reap his reward. He then "ascends" and is able to move on to a higher level of existence.

A character always knows what he wants, but hardly ever what he needs. In the end, the character usually gets close to what he wants and chooses the need instead. For example, in *Casablanca*, Bogart gets the girl—the very thing he's wanted through the entire story. But he tells her to go with her husband. His need is to get over Ingrid Bergman. When he is holding tightly to his want he is a bitter, selfish man. He even says, "I stick my neck out for no one." In the end, he risks his neck to assure that the woman he loves can leave with her husband. We know he is a better person. He has grown. He has ascended.

In *The Apartment*, Jack Lemmon gets the promotion he's been after from the beginning of the story. But he is done compromising his self-respect, and he turns down the job. He has ascended. This act helps him get his real reward, the woman he loves.

In *E.T.*, Elliott wants his friend E.T. to stay with him but helps E.T. get home. He puts the needs of his friend ahead of his own desires. It is painful for him, but it is the right thing to do. Elliott ascends to a better place through suffering ritual pain.

Most viewers of *E.T.* are unaware that they are watching the transformation of a character from a selfish child to a caring human being, but they do feel it.

Ritual pain means painfully killing off one aspect of a character's personality to make room for something new.

Character transformation and growth are some of the most powerful forms of invisible ink, and you would do well to include them in your work.

Personal hell exercise

This exercise is designed to show you how to figure out the type of ritual pain that is appropriate for your character.

In Greek mythology, Persephone, daughter of Zeus and Demeter, was abducted by Hades and taken to the underworld, the realm of the dead.

I was just reading this story and realized that all characters of change take a journey to the underworld. Characters must confront the very thing they would least like to encounter, and confronting this thing is a kind of hell. More precisely, it is their own personal hell. But through this confrontation, they are transformed.

Let's revisit our friend King Midas. If all the king wants is gold, then as a storyteller creating that story, one would have to find a way to put Midas in hell—to take him to the underworld. The storyteller grants the king his wish that everything Midas touches turns to gold. It isn't long before King Midas realizes that this blessing is a curse when he changes his beloved daughter into a golden statue. Midas learns that some things are more precious than gold. A trip to one's personal hell changes the traveler.

In the movie *Jaws*, a man is deathly afraid of the water, so where do you suppose his personal hell is? In the middle of the ocean where a vicious shark swims about, that's where.

"Snakes. Why did it have to be snakes?" says Indiana Jones in *Raiders of the Lost Ark* when he learns that he must descend into a pit of the slithering reptiles. But we know why it had to be snakes—it's because as we find out early on in the film, Indiana Jones hates snakes. To get the prize he seeks, he must take a trip to his own personal hell.

In the classic film *It's a Wonderful Life*, George Bailey wishes he had never been born. In his personal hell, he is granted the chance to see what the world would have been like without him, and it's not a pretty place.

In Alfred Hitchcock's *Shadow of a Doubt*, a young woman wishes she had more excitement in her life. She gets more excitement when her favorite uncle comes to town and turns out to be a murderer.

In *The Wizard of Oz*, Dorothy wants to run away from home, so a twister takes her far away. And, of course, all she wants to do is to get back home, because she is in her personal hell.

In *Finding Nemo*, the father desperately tries to keep his son safe by never letting him out of his sight and keeping him close to home. What happens? His son is taken away into the ocean. This is the father's personal hell.

"Of all the gin joints in all the world, she had to walk into mine," goes Bogart's famous line from the film *Casablanca*. He says this because the woman he was in love with, and wants to forget, has just come into his world. This is his personal hell.

This is one of the simplest ways to apply invisible ink to your work, but it will yield powerful results. It is a simple way to find out what your story needs to be about. Find that thing that your character would rather die than do, and then make them do it.

Of course, sometimes a character getting what they want turns into a personal hell. This is what happened for King Midas.

Here is an exercise. Write down the personal hell for the characters provided below. There is no right answer; just make sure that either the characters go to that place or do that thing they would least like or get exactly what they want and it becomes their hell.

Remember that you don't have to know how the person ends up in this place or situation for this exercise. The situation can be far-fetched or supernatural. That doesn't matter at this stage.

Example: A rich man wants nothing more than to acquire more money.

Personal hell: He finds himself penniless.

Example: A girl wants to run away from home.

Personal hell: She gets her wish and wants nothing more than to get home.

Now it's your turn.

Situation: A soldier longs for glory in battle.
Personal hell:

_____

Situation: A health enthusiast is obsessed with longevity.
Personal hell:

_____

Situation: An adventurer craves the thrill of exploration.
Personal hell:

_____

Situation: A scholar craves infinite knowledge.
Personal hell:

_____

Situation: A workaholic values career success above all.
Personal hell:

_____

Situation: A politician strives for absolute power.
Personal hell:

_____

Situation: A cop prides himself on his honesty.
Personal hell:

_____

Situation: A person won't let go of the past and move on with life.
Personal hell:

_____

THE POWER OF SACRIFICE IN STORIES

What we do for ourselves dies with us.
What we do for others is immortal.
—Often attributed to 19th-century English author Albert Pine

Sacrifice is an important part of what makes a protagonist a hero. Few of us have much respect for someone who has had things too easy. We admire struggle and sacrifice.

I remember hearing a story about a man in a Nazi death camp who volunteers to take the place of another man who is slated to be killed. The first man had a family and begged the Nazis to spare him. The second man had no family, so he sacrificed himself for the first man and his family. Few of us would do such a thing, though we all wish we would. That's what makes someone a hero—putting the needs of others before one's own.

George Bailey, in *It's a Wonderful Life,* spends his entire life sacrificing for others. We see him as a heroic figure because of his self-sacrifice.

You might think that this is visible ink, but readers and audiences are unaware of its use when it is applied skillfully.

Look at the story of the crucifixion. Jesus is suffering on the cross. It's important that this aspect of the story be relayed to us. Remember that this is the Son of God here; he can work miracles. So we might very well wonder if he suffered at all up there. His crown of thorns, his having to carry his own cross, his stab wound, are all necessary details of the narrative.

Jesus even says, "Father, why have you forsaken me?" It is important for us to know that he was not, through some miracle, spared the pain of the crucifixion. The story's power lies in the idea that he suffered just as you or I would have suffered. Like all great heroes, Jesus' suffering is for others.

And then, of course, what happens to Jesus? He rises from the grave. He ascends to heaven. He is rewarded for his pain.

According to Norse mythology, the king of the gods, Odin, gave up one of his eyes and was speared to a tree for nine days in order to gain wisdom. Attaining wisdom is never easy.

In *The Adventures of Huckleberry Finn*, Huck isn't sure if he should turn in Jim, the runaway slave. His world tells him it is a sin not to do so. But Huck has come to know and care for Jim and to see him as a human being.

At the end of the book, Huck decides that he'd rather sin than turn in his friend.

"I'll go to hell then," he says. He believes he will be punished forever for helping his friend. This is a pretty big sacrifice.

We even respect small sacrifices. One of my best friends is always willing to admit when he's wrong. He owns up to it quicker than anyone I've ever met. Not just with small things, either. How many of us are so willing to admit our mistakes and shortcomings? I'm not saying that my friend is a hero, but there is a certain amount of courage involved in being the type of person that he is. He leaves himself vulnerable emotionally, and emotional pain can be just as damaging as physical pain, sometimes more.

In *Terminator 2*, the robot from the future sacrifices himself for the good of humanity. This once-murderous machine is now a hero.

All characters of change have to die in some way, even if it's an emotional death, so that they can be resurrected.

By applying enough pressure and heat, a storyteller can change a lump of coal into a diamond.

FROM BUTTERFLY TO CATERPILLAR

If once you start down the dark path, forever will it dominate your destiny.
—Yoda, *The Empire Strikes Back*

Characters don't always change for the better. Some stories are about how people are corrupted—how angels fall.

In *The Godfather*, Michael Corleone starts off as a virtuous man—a war hero, no less. When he tells his fiancée, Kay, about his family's criminal behavior, he explains, "That's my family, Kay, not me." He is above all of this.

What is the ritual pain that begins his change? His father is shot. Michael may not approve of his family's business, but he does care for them.

His change is slow initially. First, he protects his father while the men who shot him try to finish him off. As an audience we can understand that. Who wouldn't protect someone they love from killers?

Then Michael decides that he wants to kill the men who shot his father. When he does kill them, it is not justice, it is revenge. Michael's father was not killed, only wounded.

That might not make much difference in some story realities, but it does in this one. We know this because in the opening scene Michael's own father tells us so. He defines the difference between justice and revenge when a man comes to him asking him to kill the two men who nearly raped his daughter.

BONASERA
What do you want of me? I'll give you
anything you want, but do what I ask!

> DON CORLEONE
> And what is that, Bonasera?

BONASERA whispers into the DON's ear.

> DON CORLEONE
> No. You ask for too much.

> BONASERA
> I ask for justice.

> DON CORLEONE
> The Court gave you justice.

> BONASERA
> An eye for an eye!

> DON CORLEONE
> But your daughter is still alive.

So as an audience we know when Michael has crossed onto the "dark path." And we have seen how someone can be seduced into this world. The angel has fallen.

Because the scene with Don Corleone and Bonasera is the first scene in the film, it becomes invisible ink. The audience has no idea that this scene will help them understand the rest of the film. Like all forms of invisible ink, it works on a subconscious level.

Flip-flops

When I say flip-flops I don't mean shoes. "Flip-flops" is the name that I give characters who are opposites, but exchange character traits.

Oscar and Felix of Neil Simon's play *The Odd Couple* are probably the most famous flip-flops. One is clean and prissy while the other is sloppy and gruff. Their marriages have broken up and they are thrown together as roommates. They are extreme opposites, which offers the best opportunity for conflict and, therefore, comedy. Their ritual pain is having to live with one another.

By the end of the story we have seen why both of their marriages failed. This pairing is a replay, or a clone, of each of their marriages. But it has also changed both characters. Both are a little more aware of their respective faults. They could each stand to be a little bit like the other.

In fact, the last messy thing Oscar does is tell his poker guests to watch their cigarette ashes. He says, "This is my house, not a pigsty." This is a huge change from the Oscar at the opening of the play.

Another classic example is *The African Queen*. In that film, Humphrey Bogart plays a crusty, hard-drinking boat captain, while Katharine Hepburn plays his flip-flop, a stuffy religious matron who detests vulgar vices such as demon rum. These two share little in common except the small boat they are trapped on together.

Through the ritual pain of having to make their way down a treacherous river together, they both become fuller people. Each has something the other is lacking, and by exchanging traits they become whole.

Sometimes only one of the characters needs to change, and the other is the catalyst for that change, such as in *Beauty and the Beast*. When the Beast changes enough on the inside to earn the love of a woman, he changes on the outside from a beast to a handsome man. The change is only an external manifestation of what is going on internally.

Shrek turns this idea on its green funnel-shaped ear, but it is still the same story. Shrek is completely comfortable with who he is; it is the Princess who must change.

Characters who don't change

Do characters always need to change? No, they don't. But you always have to remember what your armature is and why you are telling the story. Let that make the decision for you. What is the best way to dramatize your point?

This is not exactly the story of an individual who doesn't change, but it illustrates my point quite well, I think: When I was a kid, I learned a lot about story structure by watching old reruns of Rod Serling's *The Twilight Zone*. There is one episode called "It's a Good Life." In it, an evil five-year-old boy, who has the power to read minds and do just about anything else, has the small farm town of Peaksville, Ohio, held captive. For all intents and purposes, the rest of the world has ceased to exist.

The few people left in the town walk on eggshells so as not to suffer the boy's wrath. They are all miserable, but they try only to say good things and think good thoughts. The boy might hear their bad thoughts, were they to have them, and kill them in some cruel fashion, like setting them on fire, or worse. He even kills a couple of "clone" animals so that we, the audience, get an idea of his power. Even the boy's parents live in fear.

One night, there is a birthday gathering for one of the townsfolk at the house of the boy. The guest of honor receives a few gifts from what can be scrounged up by his friends. The town is running low on food and other provisions and luxuries, but the boy neglects to replenish them.

The boy likes music but hates singing, and one of the gifts received by the man having the birthday is a record of his favorite singer. He wants desperately to play it, but the others warn against it. Upset, he starts in on another gift, a bottle of rye whiskey. He gets drunk and starts to complain out loud for all to hear.

The other adults are in a panic—they try to distract the boy and calm the man down, but he's having none of it. Surprisingly, the boy ignores the man's drunken rant. But the man just gets louder and more obnoxious. (We, the audience, know something bad will happen, but the storytellers drag this scene out an agonizingly long time. They understood that promising conflict was a powerful form of invisible ink.)

In a final act of defiance, the man tries to get his fellow captives to join him in a rousing chorus of "Happy Birthday." The boy loses his patience and glowers at the man.

The man's song is directed right at the boy, and it becomes clear that this is a kind of suicide. When it is clear that all of the boy's attention is on him, the man tries to get someone to come up behind the boy and kill him. He begs them to take the risk. Sure, they might be killed, but if they were to succeed, all of their misery would be over.

The people do nothing. The boy kills the man in a rather grotesque manner.

With that, the boy's father notices that his son is making it snow outside. He loses his temper because the snow will ruin the crops. He begins to yell at the boy but catches himself and tells the boy that it's good that he's making it snow.

The end.

This story is more about a situation that remains the same rather than one character, but you get the idea.

What is the armature of this story, do you think? It tells us that no one has any power over us that we don't give to them. It is better to challenge oppression and die than to live under its thumb. Gandhi brought down the British Empire by simply not acknowledging their power in his country. That's it.

The drunken man in this piece becomes the hero. He makes a sacrifice hoping that it will help those left behind. The others are seen as cowards.

So how did the storytellers get away with not changing things? For one thing, it was the best way to make the point. And for another, we saw where things could have changed but didn't. If only they had stood up to the boy—to their oppressor. The fork in the road that lets the audience know what could happen is a kind of invisible ink.

The ending with the snow is important because we see that things are going to continue to be the same—"and ever since that day."

KILLING THE PROTAGONIST

> *A man who has nothing he would die for isn't fit to live.*
> —*Martin Luther King, Jr.*

If you can have your protagonist make the ultimate sacrifice, that's great. But make sure they finish their story first. What I mean is, if you kill the character in the middle of their journey, it isn't satisfying.

One of the most famous protagonist deaths is that of Janet Leigh in *Psycho*. I've heard much talk about how shocking that death was to people at the time, and how it was so groundbreaking. I'm sure it was, but Mr. Hitchcock and screenwriter Joseph Stefano still played by the rules. Janet Leigh's character was done with her story.

In *Psycho*, Janet Leigh plays a woman, Marion Crane, who steals money from her boss. She skips town and winds up at the Bates

Motel where she meets Norman. Norman makes them sandwiches that they eat in a back room of the motel. There they have this conversation about Norman's situation with his "mother."

> MARION
>
> Why don't you go away?

> NORMAN
>
> To a private island, like you?

> MARION
>
> No, not like me.

> NORMAN
>
> I couldn't do that. Who'd look after her? She'd be alone up there. The fire would go out. It'd be cold and damp like a grave. If you love someone, you don't do that to them even if you hate them. You understand that I don't hate her—I hate what she's become. I hate the illness.

> MARION
>
> Wouldn't it be better—if you put her—someplace—?

Norman's demeanor darkens. He leans forward.

> NORMAN
>
> You mean an institution? A madhouse! People always call a madhouse "someplace," don't they? "Put her in—someplace."

> MARION
>
> I—I'm sorry. I didn't mean it to sound uncaring.

NORMAN

What do you know about caring? Have you ever seen the inside of one of those places? The laughing and the tears—and the cruel eyes studying you. My mother there! But she's harmless! Wh—she's as harmless as one of those stuffed birds!

MARION

I am sorry. I only felt—it seems she's hurting you. I meant well.

Marion is more than a little spooked by his personality transformation.

NORMAN

People always mean well! They cluck their thick tongues and shake their heads and suggest, oh so very delicately—! [He sits back. The storm is over. Gently:] Of course, I've suggested it myself. But I hate to even think about it. She needs me. It—it's not as if she were a—a maniac—a raving thing. She just goes a little mad sometimes. We all go a little mad sometimes. Haven't you?

MARION
(her concern relaxed)
Yes. Sometimes just one time can be enough. Thank you.

NORMAN

"Thank you, Norman."

MARION

Norman.

> NORMAN
>
> Oh, you're not—you're not going back to your room already?
>
> MARION
>
> I'm very tired. And I have a long drive tomorrow—all the way back to Phoenix.
>
> NORMAN
>
> Really?
>
> MARION
>
> I stepped into a private trap back there and I'd like to go back and try to pull myself out of it before it's too late for me to.

She stands to go.

At the end of this scene, Marion has decided to give back the money. She is a better person now, so although we may be shocked that she is killed, we do not feel cheated.

Thelma, in *Thelma and Louise*, takes on some of the traits of Louise and becomes a stronger person. Her thematic journey is over and it is okay if she dies. We may be sad, but again, we do not feel cheated.

Billy Wilder killed a few protagonists in his day. In *Sunset Boulevard*, Joe Gillis is killed off at the end, after he has made his transformation for the better. Few people have written a script as well-constructed as *Sunset Boulevard*—with, of course, the exception of Wilder himself.

In *Ace in the Hole* (aka *The Big Carnival*), Kirk Douglas plays a down-and-out reporter who finds a way to keep a man trapped in a cave in order to milk the story for as long as he can. He wants to be back on top again. He wants a Pulitzer Prize.

The reporter convinces others to go along with his plan, all for their own selfish reasons, including the engineer in charge of digging the man out. Eventually the man gets sick, and it becomes clear he will die. This starts to change the reporter: he starts to feel guilty about what he's done, and now there is no time to get the man out.

The reporter ends up being stabbed in the belly (you'll have to see the film to see how). Instead of tending to his own wounds, he rushes to a church to get a priest to give the trapped man his last rites before he dies. He also confesses to what he's done, before he himself dies.

By not tending to his own wounds, he sacrificed his own life so that the other man could have his last rites. We know that the reporter was a better human being when he died than he was at the story's start.

What about *Butch Cassidy and the Sundance Kid*? After all, they don't get better before they die. That is true; they don't. But there is that fork in the road where they could go straight. They even try it, but it's not for them.

Before the escape to Bolivia, they are pursued by a super-posse that is almost supernatural. This could easily be seen as Death pursuing them. If they don't change their ways eventually, Death will catch up to them. They refuse to change with the times and choose to go out in a blaze of glory. As with the episode of *The Twilight Zone* mentioned before, it is important to see that there was another road that was not taken.

CHAPTER V

Tell the Truth

- Iron and silk: Dual forces that shape compelling narrative
- Drama in real life
- The myth of genre
- Climax
- Supporting plots (subplots)
- Servant, not master

We must never forget that art is not a form of propaganda;
it is a form of truth.
—John F. Kennedy

If you take nothing else away from this book, remember always to tell the truth, the whole truth, and nothing but the truth. If you do this always, you will be a master storyteller. However, this is much harder than it sounds.

What does it mean to tell the truth when writing fiction? For one thing, it is not about sticking with facts. Storytellers are not concerned with facts, just truth. Sometimes facts can even get in the way of the truth.

When you are watching a horror movie and you know that the girl in the tank top and panties shouldn't go into the basement alone, and you know she has other options but she goes into the basement anyway—that's a lie. It only happened because the storytellers wanted it to happen, not because it was a logical thing a reasonable person would do.

On the other hand, if the girl does everything you would do and is even a little smarter than you are, but the monster gets her anyway—now, *that's* scary.

You want to see truth in fiction? Watch Jimmy Stewart's breakdown in *It's a Wonderful Life*, just before he decides to kill himself. It's about as real and truthful as anything you'll ever see on film. Capra is known for being lighthearted, but when he got dark, he always told the truth. If you want to affect people deeply, tell the truth.

Remember in *Big* when Tom Hanks has gotten his wish and has become an adult? Remember his first night away from home in the sleazy hotel? He cried. This is a comedy, right? But when Hanks cries in that scene, nobody's laughing. In fact, it's painful to watch. The filmmakers played the truth of the scene.

The Donner Party was a group of pioneers in the 1840s who got snowed in while they were crossing the mountains and resorted to cannibalism to survive. This is not light subject matter. Charlie Chaplin read about this incident and thought, *Now, that's funny!*

The Donner Party inspired one of Chaplin's most famous scenes from one of his most famous films. In *The Gold Rush*, he plays a man trapped in a small cabin in the snow along with another unfortunate soul. They are starving. And even though some humor comes out of the situation, you never forget that these men are truly hungry.

With nothing left to eat, Chaplin cooks, and serves up, his leather shoe. Chaplin treats the shoe like a spaghetti dinner. He eats it like he's eating a fine meal. He makes the tragic funny. I'm not the first to say it, but the truth is funny.

Raiders of the Lost Ark has a great example of truth in it. There is a scene in which a scary opponent who dazzles us with dangerous-looking swordsmanship confronts Indiana Jones. I remember sitting in the theater on the edge of my seat, expecting an exciting action sequence. But instead, Indy calmly pulls out his gun and shoots the man dead. Anyone who saw that in the theater remembers the uproar of laughter that followed. Why was it so funny? It was the truth. It was the most logical thing for Indiana to do.

On the old *Batman* television show, the villains would always construct some Rube-Goldberg-like contraption to kill Batman. Even little kids wondered why no one ever pulled out a gun and shot him. It was a lie, and we all knew it.

Lying is visible ink. It is easy for the audience to see, and therefore it doesn't work.

Roseanne changed the face of television because she refused to lie on her show. She played the first "real" mother on television.

The film *Election* has some amazingly honest work in it. In one scene, a girl gives a speech at a school assembly, a speech that is so honest about how most of us felt about high school that it seems like she's reading from your own diary.

In that same film Matthew Broderick has a scene where he is preparing for a sexual escapade by washing his genitals in the tub. Few of us would admit to doing such a thing in public, but a theater full of people will howl with the laughter of recognition. The film was raw with the honesty of human behavior.

Most writers are afraid to put something so personal down on paper. We think that it is a window into our own personal lives, and we don't want to be judged by it. But here's the big secret—we are all the same. The more you dip into your own behavior, good or bad, the more others will see themselves and you will fade into the background.

Several decades after World War II, color movie footage of Hitler was discovered. Some people thought it shouldn't be shown because it humanized a monster. But that is what makes Hitler a monster—he was a human being, not some creature from outer space. It makes a much stronger point not to shy away from that fact. It means if we are not careful, we may produce another monster.

It is the same with a hero. If you can show that a hero had fears, doubts, and human foibles but did a heroic thing anyway, it makes him all the more heroic.

The worst of us has good in him, and the best of us has some bad. That is a truth that many of us want to deny, but as storytellers it is the truth we must illuminate.

The truth will always be sadder, happier, funnier, scarier, and more profound than the best lie. More importantly, the audience never "sees" it, but they do feel it.

IRON AND SILK: DUAL FORCES THAT SHAPE COMPELLING NARRATIVE

When form predominates, meaning is blunted; but when content predominates, interest lags. But the genius comes in when both of these things fuse.
—Legendary graphic designer Paul Rand

I was once asked to read a screenplay as a favor. This script was meant for a big-budget blockbuster. It was full of explosions, fight sequences, chases, and over-the-top action.

I was bored. There was no reason to care about what was happening or who it was happening to.

When I told this young writer that his story lacked a reason to care, he pointed to all of the action and spectacle as evidence that I was wrong. I talked until I was blue in the face trying to explain that the audience needed a reason to care, but he had no idea what I was talking about. Many storytellers make this mistake: he had leaned too heavily into what I am calling the *Iron* of the story.

Iron symbolizes the external facets of storytelling. The high-octane action sequences and set pieces. Shootouts with guns or high-tech blasters or high-speed car chases or space battles or spectacular stunts or breathtaking special effects sequences or fist fights are the kinds of things that I would describe as Iron.

These things, if done well enough, may sometimes engage an audience, but seldom will Iron move them on a deep level. Stories with an overabundance of Iron lack emotion.

There are other storytellers who lean into emotions, tone, and mood so heavily that there appears to be no story at all. These stories lean too heavily on what I call the *Silk* of the story. Nothing happens.

Silk embodies the subtle and internal dimensions of storytelling. It delves into characters' emotions or the emotional interactions between characters. And often these storytellers make mood the primary element of their storytelling. Their stories lack form.

This reminds me of something the legendary graphic designer Paul Rand once said: "Without form, there's no content. A work of art is realized when form and content are indistinguishable. When form predominates, meaning is blunted. When content predominates, interest lags. But the genius comes in when both of these fuse."

He could so easily have used the terms Iron and Silk. The true enchantment of storytelling lies in orchestrating the balance between Iron and Silk and recognizing that neither force thrives in isolation. Putting too much focus on either Iron or Silk jeopardizes a story's resonance, while balancing Iron and Silk creates harmony.

Since discovering this concept, I have made certain observations about what kinds of people lean more into one camp or the other when telling stories.

Actors, dancers, visual artists, poets, playwrights, and literature majors tend to fall more on the Silk side of things. They tend to put a lot more emphasis on character, the beauty of words, scenery, mood, and theme. Plot is seen by many of these people as cheap.

Films and books that are more Silk usually do better among critics and intellectuals, but they seldom bring in a wide audience. They are often called "character-driven." Critics will often believe that these stories are too "smart" for the masses. "Too cerebral," they might say.

Video gamers, mainstream comic book readers or creators, and action film fans tend to fall into the Iron category.

Stories with an emphasis on the visceral tend to do better with audiences. This is why the summer film releases are big-budget special effects extravaganzas. People have fun going to films like this, but they don't expect to get caught up emotionally in the content—and they seldom are, other than an "Ooh," an "Ahh," or a "Wow—that blowed up real good!"

I like to see a good explosion as much as the next guy, but I want to care about what or who is blowing up. In *Jaws*, the shark is blown up at the end, but it matters story-wise, and its one explosion has more impact than ten explosions in other films. Storytellers often feel that you either have one kind of story or another, but it is the balance that gets you the best of both worlds—an engaging story to watch or read that has resonance for the audience.

Actors often talk about giving characters vulnerability. I think this is just another way of talking about the internal, emotional life of a character. Without this quality, characters are caricatures instead of fully realized human beings.

The character of Quint in *Jaws* is a virtual parody of a salty old sailor (though well written and performed) until he delivers a speech about a terrifying experience he had with a shark attack. At that moment, a character who had shown nothing but a crusty exterior opens up and becomes human. This combination of Iron and Silk traits in the character tells the truth about being a human being. One without the other is a lie, and we know it. We feel it.

Storytellers who focus almost exclusively on the Iron elements of their story think if they make a big enough event occur then they will have a big reaction. But events themselves mean almost nothing.

Let's take, for instance, the simple action of one person handing another person an apple. This is a nothing event. Unless, of course, the characters happen to be in the garden of Eden. Then the passing of that Apple has impact. Or imagine the passing of an apple from one character to another, but this time the story is *Snow White* and the apple is a poisonous one being handed to an innocent young girl by an evil witch in disguise.

Or let's take a real-life example of one person handing an apple to another person and having that Apple means so much more than just being an apple. I once saw a documentary about a woman who survived a Nazi death camp. She said that the men were separated from the women, but every now and then each group could get a glimpse of the other through a fence. This woman was in love with a man who was on the other side of that fence, and one day he passed her an apple. She said that she couldn't remember the last time she had seen an apple. Because the people in these camps were given a bare minimum of food, this also meant that instead of eating the apple himself he gave it to the woman he loved. He sacrificed his own well-being for her in an act of selfless love.

In all of these examples the action is the same: Character A hands Character B an apple. That is an Iron element. It is completely external. But each incident is different because of the internal invisible element. This is the Silk. This is where all of the emotion comes from. The external element is incidental.

When one of my best friends was dying in a hospital because of an aneurysm, he was being watched for 72 hours on the very slim chance that he might regain consciousness. We were told that even if he did regain consciousness he would not be the same person. There was too much brain damage.

Friends and family sat in a waiting room with other friends and families of people with traumatic head injuries. At one point a woman ran out of one of the room. She had tears in her eyes and a smile on her face as she shouted with glee to her group, "She wiggled her toe! She wiggled her toe!" I took it to mean that this meant her loved one was not completely brain dead. This event gave that group hope. Wiggling a toe is a very small event if it is only an Iron event, but paired with the Silk of the high stakes and emotion the Iron becomes much more powerful. The small event becomes a much bigger event.

As I stated earlier, *Jaws* has just one explosion which, by itself, would have meant nothing. It is only Iron. But because the protagonist has been battling the shark and his own fears for most of the story, that explosion becomes an element of Silk. This is a man conquering his fear. An explosion, no matter how big, is no more important than one character handing an apple to another, unless it is infused with Silk.

There are stories where big things happen. How many times have you experienced a story where characters die and it means nothing? It's just an element of the plot. Arguably nothing is bigger than a person's death unless we are talking about the number of people killed. There are plenty of big-budget movies with a high body count, but those stories elicit no deep feelings in the audience because there is no Silk.

You have more than likely heard that conflict can be broken down into three categories: Man Against Man; Man Against Nature; Man Against Himself.

Going back to *Jaws* once again, I have seen the plot described as Man Against Nature. Is it? I think that is only an Iron view of the story's conflict. You could accurately describe the Jaws rip-offs as Man Against Nature, as they had no characters of change—no armature. But *Jaws* has a solid armature. *Jaws* is about a man facing his fear and conquering it. I would say the conflict in *Jaws* is Man Against Himself.

Moby Dick has also been described by some as Man Against Nature. This description totally ignores Captain Ahab's obsession with the white whale and how that obsession eventually kills him. The whale is only an external manifestation of Ahab's internal conflict. Iron and Silk are working together here.

There is no reason that the other two types of Iron conflicts listed above can't include Man Against Himself. In fact, to be full, they should.

Things that affect a character physically are Iron and are visible ink. How the character feels about them is Silk and invisible ink. If you can strike a balance between these two elements, your story stands a better chance of resonating with audiences.

Remember that the Iron conflict forces the protagonist to deal with their Silk conflict. It is the external pressure that makes a diamond out of a lump of coal.

The interplay of Iron and Silk not only molds narratives but profoundly influences the audience's connection.

Consider the classic film *Casablanca*, which balances both Silk and Iron components very well. It has a solid plot that ties in closely with the humanistic elements of the story. Achieving this balance gives stories a resonance that helps one reach a broader audience.

Another film classic, *It's a Wonderful Life,* makes great use of Silk as it explores the internal emotional life of depression and disappointment of its protagonist George Bailey. It also has a strong plot, or Iron, component. Virtually every classic has close to equal parts of Iron and Silk elements.

The Omaha Beach sequence of *Saving Private Ryan* was hailed by audiences and critics as being one of the most realistic war depictions in the history of film. Was it the great special effects that made it so? I don't believe so. The sequence contains both Iron and Silk elements.

When the sequence opens, Tom Hanks is having tremors, an external indication of his inner emotional condition. Other men on the Higgins boats begin to vomit from seasickness and nervous tension.

Before one shot is fired, we are already an uneasy audience. There is a sense of dread.

When the boats hit the beach, the men are riddled with bullets. How many times have we seen people being killed on film? Why is it that these deaths seemed to affect us more than most? It's because we know how these men felt before they died—their abject terror.

I know people who are usually energized by depictions of violence on screen but were mortified by these scenes of death.

In one shot, a soldier wanders back and forth in the mayhem, looking for his missing arm. In another, a man with his insides exposed cries out for his mother as he lies dying. Although full of action, this is no action film.

This film is "realistic" because it is honest about the emotional impact of violence as well as the physical effects. I have seen actual footage of D-Day with men falling down dead, and it seems less real than the war depictions in *Saving Private Ryan*. Why? It's because the footage is an incomplete picture.

Seeing a man fall over dead without knowing anything about him has less impact. *Saving Private Ryan* gives one a sense of what it might have felt like to be there.

Here's a good way to think of it: If a good friend of yours says to you, "There was a really bad car accident on the freeway yesterday," you might have some interest. On the other hand, if she says, "I was in a really bad car accident yesterday," your interest is much greater.

The first statement is all Iron; the second contains both Iron and Silk components. It involves emotion because you care about the person in the story.

I don't like everything about James Cameron's *Titanic*, but he does in that film exactly what I did with the car wreck example. At the beginning of the film (in the present day) he has a man explain, in Iron terms, what happened to the ill-fated ship after it hit the iceberg and how it sank. Later in the film we see characters we care about going through the experience. We get a sense of what it might have felt like to be on that sinking ship. This is the Silk that gives this event meaning, depth, and emotion.

Iron traits are anything that moves the story forward externally. For example, Character A, a policeman, finds out that the murderer in the case he's investigating is another cop. That is an Iron element.

The murdering cop is Character A's best friend and once risked his life to save Character A. This is a Silk element. It is the balance of these two elements that creates dramatic tension and keeps an audience interested. It keeps their brains working: What is Character A going to do? It creates depth.

Remember that the facts are not necessarily the truth. The cold fact that the *Titanic* sank says little about the truth of the experience. You don't have to take my word for this concept of Iron and Silk story elements. Listen to how people talk about stories they read, watch, and write. They will more than likely fall into one camp or the other and downplay the importance of the opposite element. They will be all-plot-and-action or all-character-and-mood.

The dance of Iron and Silk is a nuanced art demanding mastery. By comprehending the essence of Iron's external might and Silk's internal depth, you can weave narratives that not only captivate and inspire but also leave an enduring mark. Whether it unfolds on the silver screen, takes center stage, graces the pages, or adorns comic book panels, the interplay of Iron and Silk shapes narratives that transcend time, leaving an indelible imprint on those who encounter them. Look for ways to balance the Iron and Silk elements in your stories and watch as this form of invisible ink takes your stories to the next level.

DRAMA IN REAL LIFE

In 1968, sparked by the assassination of Martin Luther King Jr., an elementary school teacher from the all-white town of Riceville, Iowa, tried an exercise to teach her young students about prejudice. The exercise became an annual event.

She first asked the kids what it meant to be prejudiced. They all knew what it meant and that it was bad.

Then she told them that people with brown eyes were better than those with blue eyes. Using the tried-and-true stereotypes of racism, she said that blue-eyed people were lazy and stupid.

The blue-eyed kids were to be shunned for the entire school day. They were not to be played with or spoken to. They could not use the drinking fountain and were not allowed to use the playground equipment at recess.

In contrast, the brown-eyed kids were given second helpings at lunch and an extra five minutes of playtime at recess. They were, in every way, treated better than the blue-eyed kids.

Needless to say, the blue-eyed kids had an awful day. Their brown-eyed classmates made life hell for them. They resorted to name-calling and teasing of those who were, just the day before, their friends.

The next day, the teacher told the children that she had lied about brown-eyed people being better, and that the reverse was true.

The blue-eyed children, now believing they were superior, behaved as their brown-eyed counterparts had the day before.

At the end of the second day, she told her students why she had put them through this painful experience.

Now, when they were asked about prejudice, these children understood prejudice and its evils intimately. These young people had been transformed forever. When they are interviewed about the experience as adults, they describe it as life-changing. They also say it was worth the pain they went through.

Their teacher had told them about how bad prejudice is, but apparently the telling lesson did not take. You can see how experiencing rather than telling is what transformed these children through ritual pain. Remember, drama is a way of getting across an intellectual idea emotionally. That is exactly what happened here.

When film of the elementary school teacher's exercise is shown to adults, they learn all of the lessons the kids did, but without having to go through the experience themselves.

This is what makes drama so powerful—it is a way for people to experience things without actually experiencing them.

Your responsibility as a storyteller is to be a good teacher, not a good preacher. If you only talk about what you want to say, you are proselytizing. But if you show your audience through demonstration, the lesson will be learned, seemingly, on its own. Not only that, but your audience will learn it more thoroughly.

That is why here, in this book, I use so many stories to make my points. I want you to make the observations yourself, with my guidance.

There is more to this remarkable story, by the way. The teacher, Jane Elliot, suffered greatly for her actions. She was called a "nigger-lover" and received death threats from angry parents and townspeople. Her own children became the targets of violence perpetrated by other kids.

Through all of this, she kept doing what she thought was right.

She kept right on doing her exercise.

She made personal sacrifices for the greater good. This is the definition of a hero in life as well as drama.

Every element of drama has its real-life counterpart. Try to notice the invisible ink in life as well as in fiction.

THE MYTH OF GENRE

Living with dyslexia, I've come to appreciate the intricate tapestry of life through a unique lens—one that often blurs the lines between what society deems as separate categories. Take "genre," for instance. It's a term that partitions storytelling into neat, easily digestible boxes based on surface-level traits. But dyslexia, a companion of mine, propels me away from these artificial divisions, urging me to see not the walls but the bridges that connect disparate elements into a unified narrative. This is what I believe storytelling should be: an intricate web of interconnected emotions, experiences, and ideas that defy mere categorization.

It's fascinating to note that Leonardo da Vinci, a man widely considered one of history's greatest polymaths, is now believed by some scholars to have been dyslexic. Da Vinci once advised, "Study the science of art. Study the art of science. Develop your senses—especially learn how to see. Realize that everything connects to everything else." In this profound reflection, Da Vinci encapsulates the essence of what storytelling means to me. Just as da Vinci wasn't just about painting or inventing stuff, I'm not just a storyteller stuck in one kind of tale. My style? It's all about seeing how everything—emotions, experiences, you name it—ties together.

So, let's take this journey together. In the pages that follow, I invite you to join me in tearing down the walls of genre so you can experience storytelling as it ought to be—limitless, inclusive, and deeply human. Because when the final page is turned or the credits roll, a story's true measure isn't the setting or the spectacle, but the resonant emotional odyssey it inspires.

Genre is visible. People know if they are watching a western or science fiction. But invisible ink is about the inner workings of story, not the costumes the characters wear.

To the people who know me, I am the guy who doesn't like most new movies or TV series. People rack their brains trying to figure out what it is I do like and why. They think it might be subject matter or a certain kind of tone or maybe a particular genre. But there is always some wild card film that blows their theory.

Among people I work with, I am known as a person who can go easily from writing one genre to another. They can't figure out how I do it. It's simple. I just try to tell a story and tell it well. That is the same thing I want from other storytellers as well.

I believe that thinking of stories in genre terms only makes one think of how stories are different from one another instead of what they all have in common. Good drama doesn't respect the boundaries of genre. It doesn't care if someone rides a horse, a car, or a spaceship, as long as you care about the rider.

Genre is concerned with the external. Some stories have been told in completely different genres with only cosmetic changes. Akira Kurosawa's *Hidden Fortress*, a samurai movie, became the basis for the first Star Wars film. Another Kurosawa film, *Seven Samurai*, became a western.

Kurosawa himself took William Shakespeare's *King Lear* and set it in feudal Japan. Patrick Stewart took the same story and set it in nineteenth-century Texas for his television production *King of Texas*.

The classic musical *West Side Story* is *Romeo and Juliet* updated and set in the world of rival street gangs in 1950s New York.

The John Wayne western *Red River* is a retelling of the classic sea epic *Mutiny on the Bounty*. Same story, different genre.

Genre is irrelevant to the dramatist. A dramatist should only be concerned with drama. If one genre can help you tell your story better than another, use it. No genre is better or worse than another.

If you think about it, *Jaws* is just a monster movie. And, like a lot of monster movies, incidental characters are picked off as our hero tries to stop the creature. But somehow, the film transcends genre. It's successful because it has an armature and a character that changes in the course of the movie.

Lots of films came out after *Jaws* that tried to replicate its success by emulating its Iron elements. One film used an orca whale in place of a shark, and another used a mutated bear.

None of these films went below the surface to understand why *Jaws* had resonance.

Terminator and *Aliens* are also just monster movies on the outside; what sets them apart are their strong armatures.

This happens in literature as well. No one ever says that *1984* is just a science fiction novel. Or that *Animal Farm* is a kid's book because it has talking animals. Nor do they say the same of *Gulliver's Travels* because it uses fantasy.

Is *Star Wars* sci-fi or fantasy or action? If it is sci-fi, does it have anything in common with *Alien*? What do *E.T.* and *2001: A Space Odyssey* have in common? What are the similarities between *Terminator 2* and *Galaxy Quest*? Indeed, those films have little in common.

We have also prescribed a hierarchy to genre stories: "This is a costume drama; it must have more to say than a sci-fi story." That, of course, is not the truth.

When Clint Eastwood made *Unforgiven*, it was different from most westerns before it because it was more concerned with theme than with props, setting, costumes, and stereotypes. It transcended genre.

Fed up with the restrictions enforced on him by networks and advertisers, Rod Serling stopped writing the prestigious teleplays for live television for which he was famous. When he announced that he would be doing a fantasy show, many thought he had given up on doing "serious work" for television.

Mr. Serling knew something the executives didn't. "I knew I could have Martians say things that Democrats and Republicans couldn't," he said. He was able to use the prejudice of genre hierarchy to his advantage.

He wrote fantastical stories about real human issues without any flack from advertisers, and audiences always knew what he was saying.

We all have a fondness for a particular motif. I like the clothes and cars from the mid-twentieth century. I have a visceral response to those things when I see them in movies. That doesn't make the film good.

More importantly, other people may not share my appreciation for these things, so as a storyteller, I must speak to them on a deeper level. The armature must be so strong that it makes the story universal and makes the genre inconsequential.

As a storyteller, you should be aware of the genre in which your story will most likely be viewed. Outwardly, it should belong to a recognized genre so that it will be easier to sell and to market. Only you need to know that you've transcended the genre. Your audience will know it, too; they just won't know that they know.

Related to this topic is the idea that one medium is superior to another—live theater is more artistic than cinema—or that novels are inherently better than comic books, or movies are better than television.

These are all just mediums that can be used to tell stories, and that is all. Each has its own strengths, and it is up to you to use the strengths of whichever medium you choose to help tell your story.

If you want to test this idea, read the graphic novels (comic books) *Maus* and *Maus II* by Art Spiegelman. *Maus* was the first comic book ever to win a Pulitzer Prize. A special category had to be created so that the book qualified.

Will Eisner's graphic novels are also worth your time. I'm sure that if he told stories in another medium, everyone would know his name. In fact, the top award in comics bears his name. He has won several of these awards, by the way.

Early in the days of movies, they were regarded as a cheap, dirty little entertainment. Most "legitimate" actors avoided the "flickers" altogether. But there were a few pioneers who saw the power of the medium and learned to use it to tell stories.

D. W. Griffith was the first filmmaker to use crosscutting—that is, cutting between one scene and another to build tension. When others voiced their concerns, saying that it might confuse the audience, he said, "If Dickens can do it, so can I."

Don't let your medium or your genre stop you from telling a good story.

CLIMAX

One of my students once asked me, "What about climax?" At first, I didn't understand the question. What about climax? I thought it was pretty self-explanatory. It's the one thing everyone knows about story structure—that at the end, there's a climax. But I thought about it more and realized: A climax is the bringing together of the Iron and Silk elements that shows the character's change, or lack thereof. We can see how much a character has changed based on how they respond when the pressure is on.

At the climax of *E.T.*, the government agents try to capture the alien, and Elliott helps him go home. Elliott does this even though it hurts him.

Going back to sacrifice, one of the things sacrifice does is allow audience members to see the sincerity of a character's change. It gives them a yardstick by which to measure growth.

In *Tootsie,* Dustin Hoffman could continue lying about being a woman, but at the climax he has grown enough to tell the truth.

At the climax, he reveals himself to be a man on live television. He does this despite the possibility of a lawsuit by his employers and the alienation of the woman he has fallen in love with. But he is an honest man now, and we see it through his extreme actions.

In *Casablanca,* Bogart does precisely what he said he wouldn't do and he "sticks his neck out" for others by killing a man and giving up the woman he loves. Nothing forces him to do this except his own growth.

In *Jaws,* the climax occurs when the protagonist is alone on a sinking boat as the shark makes its way toward him. But he has the courage to do what he does. His fear is gone.

The climax of the *Twilight Zone* episode mentioned earlier takes place when the man having the birthday challenges the others to kill the kid with the powers. He makes a sacrifice, but since the others don't respond to his call, it is for nothing. But we can measure their lack of change by their inaction.

The climax of the play *A Doll's House* is Nora's change. She stands up to her husband in a way she never would have done at the beginning of the play.

Simply put, the climax of a story puts the protagonist in an intense situation that forces a choice that shows growth or lack of growth.

This is only true of stories that transcend genre and have a solid armature.

SUPPORTING PLOTS (SUBPLOTS)

I don't like the term *subplot* because I think it confuses people. What happens is that storytellers try to include subplots to flesh out their world and make it feel full. This is never a reason to introduce a character or subordinate (sub) plot.

I like to call them supporting plots. They are there to support the main plot. Everything should hang off the same armature.

The other womanizers in *Tootsie* only exist to put pressure on Hoffman's character to see himself in another light and change. How is that subordinate to the main plot? It isn't.

What about the man who honestly falls in love with Hoffman as a woman? It shows Hoffman how his lies can hurt people deeply.

There is nothing subordinate about these plots. If you think of them as supporting plots, it will lead you down a path that supports what you are trying to say. Your world will, indeed, be fleshed out, but with things that matter.

Few can see the impact of supporting plots on the armature idea, but there they are, invisibly making stories more resonant.

SERVANT, NOT MASTER

I often have spoken to writers who say the reason they like writing is that they have so much power. If you want it to snow, you can make it snow. Or if you want to make it sunny, you can make it sunny. You can do whatever you want. You are a master of the universe. Guess what—that is not so. You are a servant to your story, not a master. Your characters, places, scenes, and sequences must be built around the armature.

In *Raising Arizona,* when the convict escapes from prison, it is raining. Why is this so? It is raining because that scene has to resemble a birth as much as possible. The mud dripping down the convict's face as he emerges from the hole, screaming, helps complete the image of a grotesque birth. The rain provides the mud, of course, but there is also thunder and lightning. There is a storm, which further signifies that something is wrong.

Think of your work as a writer more as making discoveries rather than decisions. You will then find yourself looking for things that illustrate your point. If you do this, your work will be stronger and more focused. It will elevate your work over most.

I know some storytellers who think they can buck the system. They want to bend the rules of story around what they want to do. It doesn't work. But they never seem to understand why people don't like their work. It's a pretty simple rule—if you write without a destination, it's a sure bet that you'll never get there.

CHAPTER VI

Dialogue

- Sounding natural
- Address and dismiss
- Address and explain

My barber wants to make a film. He wants to write a screenplay, so he wants to know the format. He figures that once he knows the format, he's set. There is nothing else to know, right? As he said to me, "I already know what I want people to say."

Most people are under the impression that scriptwriting is coming up with dialogue. Most critics seem to think this as well. They will go on and on about dialogue, but they know nothing about drama or how it is structured.

I feel like dialogue is talked about and written about far too often. Dialogue is the writing that people can see, so they focus on it. Of course, you know now how much more there is to story construction. But I suppose I must write a little about dialogue.

Remember that invisible ink is the writing below the surface of the words. This invisible ink keeps the audience's brains active. Subtext is a kind of invisible ink. The dialogue exchange that follows is something I heard at a friend's house, over a Christmas breakfast, between a mother and her grown daughter.

MOTHER
You sound hoarse.

DAUGHTER
Yeah, I had a cold. It's going away now.

MOTHER
You should take care of that. How long have you had it?

DAUGHTER
I'm fine. It hung on for a while. I'm fine.

MOTHER
It's going away? You taking anything for it?

DAUGHTER
I'm okay.

There is nothing unusual about this conversation. But here's the thing: The daughter's husband had recently died of AIDS. The daughter also had been diagnosed with AIDS but was not yet showing any signs of the disease. Read the exchange again with that in mind. That's subtext. That's invisible ink. Lots is being said but not spoken.

Subtext can make your scene and characters come to life on the page because it gives them an inner life and can help them become three-dimensional beings even if they are fictional. It also makes the audience participate in the storytelling as they actively decipher what the characters are really saying. This keeps the audience engaged.

A good scene is often more about what is unsaid. That's the real scene.

Subtext is a one example of well-conceived dialogue, but there are others. Dialogue is a tool, and just like any tool, you use it when you need it. It can be used to define your armature, give essential plot information, or reveal character. If it isn't doing that, it isn't doing anything.

The following scene is from *Some Like it Hot*. In this scene, we meet the two main characters. They are musicians who play in a speakeasy during Prohibition.

SOME LIKE IT HOT
Screenplay by Billy Wilder and I.A.L. Diamond, 1958

The girls have gone into a tap-dance. The captain of the chorus looks toward the bandstand, grins and winks at— JOE, the saxophone player. He winks back. JERRY, who is thumping the bass fiddle behind him, leans forward and taps Joe on the shoulder.

                    JERRY
Say, Joe—tonight's the night, isn't it?

                    JOE
(eye on tap-dancer) I'll say.

                    JERRY
I mean, we get paid tonight, don't we?

                    JOE
Yeah. Why?

He takes the mouthpiece out of his saxophone, wets the reed.

                    JERRY
Because I lost a filling in my back tooth.
I gotta go to the dentist tomorrow.

                    JOE
Dentist? We been out of work for four
months—and you want to blow your first
week's pay on your teeth?

                    JERRY

It's just a little inlay—it doesn't even have to
be gold—

                     JOE

How can you be so selfish? We owe back
rent—we're in for eighty-nine bucks to Moe's
Delicatessen—we're being sued by three
Chinese lawyers because our check bounced
at the laundry—we've borrowed money from
every girl in the line—

                    JERRY

You're right, Joe.

                     JOE

Of course I am.

This is called exposition. The scene gives us information about the financial status of these men, as well as about their personalities.

Exposition is some of the hardest writing to do. Finding a natural way to have characters speak things they already know can seem impossible at times. It is easy to do it clumsily. This is the kind of thing you should learn from observing the way others do it.

But here is a word of warning: now that you know what to look for, many of these techniques will seem obvious to you; be careful not to dismiss something because you can now see it.

SOUNDING NATURAL

Over the last few years, I have noticed that every character I read, or see in the movies or on television, sounds like a character in another movie or television show. Real people don't talk like movie people. Listen to how people speak. They didn't all grow up in your neighborhood, nor do they all have your educational background.

Because I've worked in both animation and comic books, I know a lot of illustrators. One of the things I learned is that the good ones always do life-drawings. They learn to draw the human figure from looking at a human figure. Sounds obvious, huh? Well, it's not. Many comic book artists learn from copying other artists. These people are never as good draftsmen as their life-drawing counterparts. They will often hear the advice, "Draw from life." This is good advice for us all.

When you write dialogue or anything else, think of yourself as a puppeteer. You are behind the scenes; you don't want anyone to be thinking of you. You want their attention on the puppet. Once they are thinking of you, you've lost them.

This doesn't mean you can't have a character say witty, funny, smart, profound things, but it had better be the character talking, not you.

Your job as a storyteller is to get out of the way of the story. This isn't about you. It may be about what you have to say, but it isn't about you. Let go of your ego.

ADDRESS AND DISMISS

The first time I noticed this technique, I was watching John Carpenter's *The Thing*. In the film, an alien creature with the ability to assume any form terrorizes a group of men at an isolated research base.

In this particular scene, the alien has assumed the shape of one of the men but then begins to distort. The neck stretches impossibly and tendons snap. The head detaches from the rest of the body as the other men watch in disbelief. The head, now upside down on the floor, sprouts spider's legs and grows two antennas with eyes on the ends. Even for this film, it was almost too much. They had reached the outer bounds of their reality. Just then one of the men says, "You gotta be fucking kidding."

This kind of dialogue can save you when you think you may lose your audience. Sometimes audience members need a representative within the narrative. It allows you to address and dismiss their concerns so that they can stay engrossed in the story.

A very famous address and dismiss is in *Butch Cassidy and the Sundance Kid,* when they are trying to escape the super-posse by jumping off a cliff into a river.

When Sundance admits he can't swim, Butch laughs and says, "Well, hell, the fall will probably kill you!"

This example cuts the audience off at the pass, so to speak, before they can say, "Give me a break, there is no way they could make that jump!"

In *Tootsie,* we must believe that the other characters think Dustin Hoffman is a woman. There are many comments made by other characters about how unattractive Tootsie is. This is an excellent use of address and dismiss.

All of these examples get laughs from the audience. I think it's because it's another kind of truth-telling. It's a tricky tool because it could pull people out of the scene. It is a kind of wink to the audience that lets them know the storyteller realizes that maybe she's gone too far; but when used correctly, it is seamless—invisible.

ADDRESS AND EXPLAIN

This is related to "address and dismiss" but serves a different function. The best example is in the first *Star Wars,* when Luke Skywalker sees the Millennium Falcon for the first time. After it was revealed, a hush came over the audience as they took in the magnificent ship. Then Luke exclaims, "What a piece of junk!"

The crowd erupted with laughter because that's not at all what they were thinking.

This was George Lucas's world, and we knew nothing about it. There is no way we would have known that the ship was considered a piece of junk without that clever bit of dialogue.

One of the things that drives me crazy when people talk about "good dialogue" is that they never talk about how well it's used, only how it stands out. Some of the best dialogue is quiet and subtle and reveals things about plot, theme, or character with the precision of a surgeon. Sometimes that means it's not quotable, but creating quotable dialogue is not the primary job of a storyteller.

Truly great dialogue rarely calls attention to itself. Great dialogue often works its magic invisibly.

Subtext Exercise

Here is the scene again from my Christmas breakfast, but with the subtext provided.

MOTHER

You sound hoarse.

Subtext: I'm worried that you may be very ill.

                    DAUGHTER
Yeah, I had a cold. It's going away now.
Subtext: Don't worry, I'm not dying.

                    MOTHER
You should take care of that. How long have you had it?
Subtext: I'm so worried that you might die.

                    DAUGHTER
I'm fine. It hung on for a while. I'm fine.
Subtext: I'm not dying, let's not talk about this anymore!

Notice how the dialogue itself could be read as mundane—even boring. It's what is unseen that gives the conversation its power. Now it's your turn to bring a scene to life.

Please read the following scene through:

Sarah and Molly find themselves alone together at the front of the church at their mother's casket. They nod hello to one another.

                    MOLLY
How're the kids?

                    SARAH
Grown.

                    MOLLY
Happens fast.

                    SARAH
Not so fast.

                    MOLLY
How's Kris?

SARAH

Engaged.

MOLLY

Engaged? Seems like he was just a little kid.

SARAH

Got the house all to myself now. Guess I can make that crafts room now. Big house.

MOLLY

I was sorry to hear about Roberto.

SARAH

Got your flowers.

They stare at their mother's body in the casket.

MOLLY

They did a good job. She looks good.

SARAH

She looks better than she did in the hospital.

MOLLY

I couldn't make it.

SARAH

Well, I know you couldn't get out of work.

MOLLY

I couldn't make it.

SARAH

I understand, your work is important to you.

MOLLY

I couldn't make it.

SARAH

I understand.

Now that you have read the scene, please do the exercise that follows. Write the subtext for each line in the blank spaces provided. You are welcome to do it more than once using different subtext.

Try one pass where Molly and Sarah are clearly angry at each other and another pass where they are trying to apologize to one another.

[Sarah and Molly find themselves alone together at the front of the church at their mother's casket. They nod hello to one another.]

How're the kids?
Subtext_____

SARAH

Grown.
Subtext_____

MOLLY

Happens fast.
Subtext_____

SARAH

Not so fast.
Subtext_____

MOLLY

How's Kris?
Subtext_____

SARAH

Engaged.
Subtext_____

MOLLY

Engaged? Seems like he was just a little kid.
Subtext_____

SARAH

Got the house all to myself now. Guess I can make that crafts room now. Big house.

Subtext_____

MOLLY

I was sorry to hear about Roberto.

Subtext_____

SARAH

Got your flowers.

Subtext_____

[They stare at their mother's body in the casket.]

MOLLY

They did a good job. She looks good.

Subtext_____

SARAH

She looks better than she did in the hospital.

Subtext_____

MOLLY

I couldn't make it.

Subtext_____

SARAH

Well, I know you couldn't get out of work.

Subtext_____

MOLLY

I couldn't make it.

Subtext_____

SARAH

I understand, your work is important to you.

Subtext_____

                           MOLLY

I couldn't make it.
Subtext_____

                           SARAH

I understand.
Subtext_____

You should know your characters well enough to know what they are thinking and feeling even if they aren't saying it directly.

One of my major complaints with writing is often that characters say exactly what they mean which gives the audience nothing to do but marvel at the intelligence or cleverness of the writer. It calls attention to the writer rather than the characters.

CHAPTER VII

Superior Position

- Show them once so they know

There is a distinct difference between 'suspense' and 'surprise,' and yet many pictures continually confuse the two. I'll explain what I mean. We are now having a very innocent little chat. Let's suppose that there is a bomb underneath this table between us. Nothing happens, and then all of a sudden, 'Boom!' There is an explosion. The public is surprised, but prior to this surprise, it has seen an absolutely ordinary scene, of no special consequence. Now, let us take a suspense situation. The bomb is underneath the table and the public knows it, probably because they have seen the anarchist place it there.

The public is aware the bomb is going to explode at one o'clock and there is a clock in the decor. The public can see that it is a quarter to one. In these conditions, the same innocuous conversation becomes fascinating because the public is participating in the scene. The audience is longing to warn the characters on the screen: 'You shouldn't be talking about such trivial matters. There is a bomb beneath you and it is about to explode!' In the first case we have given the public fifteen seconds of surprise at the moment of the explosion. In the second we have provided them with fifteen minutes of suspense. The conclusion is that whenever possible the public must be informed. Except when the surprise is a twist, that is, when the unexpected ending is, in itself, the highlight of the story.

—Alfred Hitchcock

Alfred Hitchcock's definition of superior position is about the best there is. It exists when the audience knows something that the characters do not know. Most of the time it's used for suspense, but not always.

In Chuck Jones's hilarious animated cartoon *Feed the Kitty*, a huge bulldog adopts a sweet little kitten. The problem, or conflict, is that the woman of the house has forbidden the dog to bring anything into the house, so he must keep his new pet a secret.

At one point in the film, the woman starts to make cookies, and unbeknownst to her, the kitten climbs into a bowl of batter set under an electric mixer. When the woman flicks the switch to mix the cookies she finds that her dog has pulled the plug. She doesn't know he's trying to save his pet and just thinks he's causing trouble. She puts the dog outside so that she can work uninterrupted. While the woman is putting the dog out, the kitten climbs out of the bowl and wanders off.

This all happens when no one is watching—except the audience. We now have superior position.

The woman returns to her cookies unaware there was ever a cat in the mixing bowl. Worried about his pet, the dog is outside looking through the window as the woman flips the mixer on. He is mortified as the beaters go to work on the batter and, he thinks, his little kitten.

I have seen this film in a movie theater, and I have rarely heard such uproarious laughter as I heard during this scene. The poor bulldog looks on in abject horror as the cookie dough is rolled out with a rolling pin, then cut by cookie-cutters, then put into an oven to bake.

Outside, the dog is a wreck. He blubbers like a baby and lies in a pool of his own tears.

Why is this so damned funny to an audience? And believe me, it is funny.

It's funny because we know the cat is okay. Imagine how people would react if they thought the cute little kitten had been beaten, cut up, and baked. It wouldn't be very funny. But just letting the audience in on the joke allowed the storytellers to put that poor dog through hell.

Even frightening experiences in our own lives can be funny in the retelling because we have a superior position over our past selves. We know that everything turned out okay.

Remember that you have this tool, and it can frighten or amuse an audience depending on how you apply it.

This kind of invisible ink is often overlooked by storytellers, but if you want to keep readers turning pages, or viewers watching, you would do well to master this technique.

Alfred Hitchcock used it to engage filmgoers throughout his fifty-year career.

SHOW THEM ONCE SO THEY KNOW

This is a great tool for storytelling. It is almost always invisible to an audience.

In the film *The African Queen*, there is a sequence in which the characters' small boat is trapped on a sandbar. Humphrey Bogart's character must get into the river and try to pull the boat free by hand. Unable to free the boat, he climbs back aboard. When Katherine Hepburn notices that Bogart has leeches on him, Bogart goes into a panic. He is deathly afraid of, and disgusted by, leeches, and he trembles in horror. He is truly shaken by this event.

Shortly after the leeches have been removed, the characters realize there is nothing they can do to free the boat by staying aboard. So Bogart must try again to free it by hand. It means he must get back into the river. You can almost feel his dread as this realization sinks in.

When he starts down into the river we know how brave he is. We know that he's facing an obstacle that is particularly large for him. It is almost like he is his own clone character. We can measure his bravery next to the fear we have seen before.

This kind of invisible ink can be used a couple of ways.

Close Encounters of the Third Kind is a film that makes use of UFOs as part of its reality. Here is a famous scene from that film.

Richard Dreyfuss is in his truck at night and he gets lost. He stops his car in the middle of the road to check his map. Behind him, we see a pair of headlights drive up. Dreyfuss waves the car around. The driver goes around Dreyfuss's truck.

Very shortly after, the scene is repeated almost exactly. Dreyfuss has stopped and is looking at his map when a pair of headlights drives up. Without looking up from his map, Dreyfuss waves the car around. Unbeknownst to him the lights behind the truck rise vertically. (Good use of superior position, by the way.) It's a creepy scene.

It works so well because we saw the previous headlights behave in a normal fashion, so now we have a comparison between what is normal and what is strange. Very smart storytelling.

The interesting thing is that most people forget about the first set of headlights altogether, but it is what makes the second pair of lights strange and fantastic.

Spielberg does the same thing in the first Jurassic Park movie. Knowing that the Tyrannosaurus rex's vision is based on motion, the Sam Neil character throws a road flare off into the distance so that the T. rex will follow the flare away from kids it's attempting to eat. His tactic works.

Shortly after this, Jeff Goldblum's character tries the same thing. He waves the flare to get the dinosaur's attention. The T. rex chases Goldblum. Then Goldblum throws the flare off to the side expecting the monster to follow—it does not. It never misses a step and continues after Goldblum.

This creates tension in the audience because we know what was supposed to happen and how it went wrong.

This kind of invisible ink is used in Pixar's *Finding Nemo*. The tough fish has a plan to escape the tank where they are kept. As he tells the other fish his plan, the filmmakers show us exactly how the plan is supposed to work, so that when it later goes wrong the audience knows where and how the plan derails.

This creates a kind of wonderful anxiety in the audience. They bite their collective nails as they follow along and the plan is carried out. Will it work?

When I was a kid, I read a lot of magazines and books about special effects, and whenever they showed a photo of a miniature they would place a quarter or some such object next to it so the reader would have a sense of scale. One could see just how small the model was because we all knew the size of a quarter.

This is akin to how the first two pigs are used in the Three Little Pigs story. As I said earlier, it is the failure of the first two pigs that allows us to measure the success of the third. In a sense, we have scale—things to compare.

We know how strange and unusual it is to have headlights float up instead of going around a car.

We feel that Jeff Goldblum is in real trouble with the T. Rex because his plan doesn't work as it should.

This form of invisible ink is often ignored by inexperienced story-crafters. They will often jump right to the third little pig, expecting the audience will "get it." They won't.

Invisible ink is all about communicating with your audience clearly and getting them to feel and think what it needs to so they will experience your story.

CHAPTER VIII

When Bad Things Happen to Good Stories

- How to translate critiques
- Judging your own work

One day I was watching *Close Encounters of the Third Kind* and I realized that it had the wrong ending. Who am I to say this? I'm just a guy who looked at the clues and saw the grammatical errors in the dramatic structure.

First, let me say that I like Spielberg. More than a few people don't like his work, but he is a master storyteller and you should learn all you can from him and use those skills to tell the stories you want to tell.

In short, CE3K is about a man, played by Richard Dreyfuss, who sees a UFO one night and becomes obsessed with seeing it again. The UFO has planted an image in his brain, and he is driven to find out what this shape means.

He begins acting so strangely that his wife takes his kids and leaves him.

When he realizes that the image in his head is Devil's Tower in Wyoming, he goes through hell and high water to get there.

I'm leaving out some details, but when he gets to Devil's Tower, he sees the UFOs and is invited to leave with the aliens. This is what he's wanted, so he leaps at the chance and boards the spaceship. It flies into the sky over the closing credits, taking Richard Dreyfuss away on a wondrous journey to parts unknown.

The End.

But this is the wrong ending.

Richard Dreyfuss has a wife and kids he's leaving behind. He didn't make a sacrifice. What he did is selfish. He has not grown from this experience at all.

There are even several clones in the film that tell you that Dreyfuss may be gone for decades. There are people returning to earth who have been missing for years. Where are their families now? Their lives will be disrupted forever. Yet Dreyfuss goes.

He even sees how upset one character is because her son was taken away from her, even for a short time.

The ending would have been stronger if Dreyfuss had to watch as the spaceship disappears into the sky while he stayed behind.

That's just my opinion, right? No, it isn't. After I noticed this problem with the film, I heard Spielberg himself say that he would have chosen a different ending now.

When he wrote the script, he didn't have a family and now he does. He said that he would make a different decision now.

Spielberg was making the mistake I see a lot of writers make. He was having the character do what he himself would have done in a given situation without really looking at what needed to happen in the story.

You are the servant of your story, not its master. You don't make decisions, you make discoveries.

Let's use another Spielberg film that I love, *Raiders of the Lost Ark*.

What could possibly be wrong with that?

A good friend and I have an ongoing argument about this film, but ultimately I think we agree. He doesn't understand how Indiana knows to close his eyes when the Ark of the Covenant is opened.

My argument is that he's been set up as an expert on the Ark, so it's no surprise that he knows what to do at the end.

First, let's look at something that could be seen as *deus ex machina*—the literal appearance of God from a box to save the day. The storytellers did a very clever thing: they planted God throughout the film, so it is not out of the blue when God shows up at the end.

When Marion first produces the headpiece to the Staff of Ra, the wind begins to blow. She is inside when this happens; yet the wind blows.

Later, when the old Egyptian man translates the markings on the headpiece, the wind blows even harder than before. Again we are inside, so wind is a little unusual.

Then it comes time to dig up the Ark. Storm clouds boil with thunder and lightning. This is real Old Testament God behavior. (By the way, there is no other use of weather in the film.)

God gets more blatant later when the Nazi's swastika is burned off the crate where the Ark is being kept. By this time, we have been primed for God's appearance, so we aren't pulled out of the story.

What's the big deal when God comes out of the box at the end?

It comes down to Indy's character change.

When the film starts, it is established that Indiana Jones does not believe in God. By the end of the film, he seems to believe in the Almighty.

None of these evidences of God are for Indy's benefit. They are never shown to him, so his change comes out of thin air. That's the *deus ex machina*: his sudden change. That's why my friend wants to know how Indy knew what to do at the end.

Albert Brooks is a hilarious filmmaker, but sometimes he makes mistakes in his storytelling. In his film *Mother*, he plays a man whose marriage has just broken up, so he goes to live with his mother to find out why he can't relate to women. He and his mother don't get along, and he figures this is where all of his woman trouble stems from.

Here's the problem: Because Albert Brooks decides to live with his mother, the conflict feels forced. The two have great, hilarious disagreements. They drive each other crazy, but one is always aware that Albert could leave anytime he wants. This takes the edge off their comedic conflict. I kept asking myself, "Why doesn't he just leave?" It isn't honest. Tell the truth, remember?

Whenever there are characters who don't want to be together, the storyteller needs to find some glue that holds them together. In *The Odd Couple*, for instance, Oscar is afraid Felix will kill himself. So, as much as his friend drives him crazy, Oscar doesn't want him to die. Felix stays because he has no place else to go. These two things are the glue that binds them together.

Mother could have used more glue. Watch it and see if you agree.

Stalag 17 is a Billy Wilder film that, even though I have it on DVD, I can't keep from watching when it comes on TV. And as much as I love Mr. Wilder's work, I think this film is flawed.

The story takes place in a German POW camp during the Second World War. The Americans imprisoned there think there is a German spy living among them in their barracks. William Holden plays Sefton, the suspected traitor. He is a wonderfully gray character, and it is easy to see why the others suspect him.

But there are two characters who seem not to serve any real function. They are comic relief, but they too often pull the focus away from the main story. Few things these characters do support the main plot. They are the fat on what is otherwise a lean script.

I have shown this film to people hoping they would enjoy it, and for many these two characters ruin the film.

You may think that I watch films looking for these types of mistakes, but I don't. After a while these things will stick out to you like a sour note to a musician.

HOW TO TRANSLATE CRITIQUES

The truth of the matter is that most people don't have the skills to articulate what is bothering them about a piece of writing. They will see everything through the lens of their tastes and their concept of drama. Rarely will they look at what you are attempting to do and be able to give unbiased advice about how to achieve it. Their comments will be subjective, not objective. Everyone who reads the work will say something different.

They will say things to make themselves sound learned. They will correct your spelling and comma placement. They will hate the main character but never tell you it's because he's just like a guy who owes them money. They will see things that are not there and never ever see the invisible ink.

So how do you sift through all of this and get to the helpful stuff? You must learn to hear what they mean, not what they say. Listen to the music, not the lyrics.

But if they say they didn't like the ending, remember what Billy Wilder said: "If there is something wrong with the third act, it is really in the first act."

Here are some hints:

- If you hear the same critique from three or more people, listen to it. But keep in mind that they might be describing the symptom rather than the disease.

- If someone doesn't understand what is going on in your story, that is worth listening to.
- If someone loses interest in your story, it is worth finding out where this happens.
- Other writers can often be the worst at giving critiques. They will try to remake you in their image: "This is how I would do it." Only they won't say that out loud.
- If you clearly communicate your story, other writers will often say that it's too blatant.

This is something I learned when I worked in animation. When you show work in progress, they will always feel obliged to tell you what's wrong with it and how to fix it. But when you show them a finished piece, they are much more accepting.

JUDGING YOUR OWN WORK

A writer is someone for whom writing is more difficult than it is for other people.
—*Thomas Mann*

Don't write for other writers. People are drawn to writing for different reasons, and many people do it to seem smart. If you have a good first act, most will never recognize it because they're not really clear on what a first act does. They know nothing about construction but will turn their noses up at the idea of it anyway. The less they know about it, the more they will object to it.

One thing I have noticed about people who are exceptional in their creative work is that they are always trying to get better. That's how they got good in the first place. These people judge themselves against their best work. They aim for the top.

Just worry about the craft, and the art will take care of itself.

The term *self-expression* has had a harmful impact on storytellers. Stories are not about the storyteller. If your focus is on yourself, then it is not on what is best for your story.

Learn to look at your work as if it isn't your work. Be as hard on yourself as you would be with anyone else.

Learn from the masters. Figure out how they did what they did, why it worked, and then apply it.

Don't be fooled by flash-in-the-pan successes, and don't try to imitate what is new and novel. If someone comes along and does something different, such as telling a story backwards or out of sequence, it doesn't mean it's going to be the way things are done from now on. How many backward movies do you want to see?

Respect your audience. It's not their job to "get it"; it's your job to communicate it to them.

Understand that you are only as good as you are today, and don't beat yourself up. You'll get better.

CHAPTER IX

Good Stories, Good Business

In 1993, there were, as I understand it, more comic books published than in any other year. Just a few short years later, so few comics were selling that many wondered if the medium would even survive. Why the big turnaround? Lack of story and story-craft.

In the world of comic books, the superstars are the artists. Most fans are initially attracted to the artwork in a book. In the early '90s, editors started letting more of these popular illustrators write as well as draw.

Some of these artists broke from the major publishers and started to produce books of their own. Understandably, these new businesses wanted people to buy their product, so they touted and promoted each book as a collector's item. This worked amazingly well.

They put out books with alternate covers. They had gold covers, silver covers, platinum covers, and glow-in-the-dark covers. The idea was to sell as many copies of a single issue as possible. Some collectors would buy ten to twenty copies of a book. This plan seemed to be working like a charm.

After a while, the speculator market dried up. I suspect they started to realize what makes Superman #1 valuable is the fact that not everyone in the world has twenty copies. And that printing the words "Collector's Item" on the cover didn't necessarily make it so.

What was the flaw in their plan? They went after buyers, not readers. Few people were actually reading these comics. Why? Few of these new companies bothered to hire professional, skilled writers. If the artist was not writing the book, he hired an old buddy from high school to do it. These "writers" had no sense of craft, and their bosses didn't care. After all, these books weren't for reading; they were for putting into plastic bags and storing in a safe place until the collector saw fit to sell them for a truckload of money.

Here's the thing: if they had tried to get people interested in the stories and characters, people may have kept buying these books, even when they realized that they wouldn't be worth a lot of money.

These companies devalued the importance of story at their peril. Now most of these companies are gone or are mere shadows of what they once were, and their comic books can be found in that purgatory of comicdom—the quarter bin. Now, just twenty-five cents buys you a "collector's item," although the printed cover price may say two dollars or more.

One of these companies put out a guide for aspiring comic-book creators. In the section on writing, they said this: "Each issue should have a simple story goal… the next step is filler." This is no exaggeration. This was virtually the entire chapter on writing stories.

These companies didn't have even a rudimentary understanding of how stories are constructed or of their purpose.

On the flip side of that same coin is this: When I was a kid, writer/artist Frank Miller was doing *Daredevil* for Marvel Comics, and I would read them in school. There was a girl in my math class who teased me for reading comics.

One day, she was bored, having finished her assignment, and she asked me if she could read one of my comics. I gave her an issue of *Daredevil*. She got caught up in the story and wanted to read more. I brought her the entire run of the series. She plowed through the books, and upon completing the last issue, requested the next. She was flabbergasted to hear she would have to wait an entire month!

Miller had crafted a book with a balance of Iron and Silk elements. There was plenty of action, but there was always an emotional component to what was happening that made me, the girl in my math class, and thousands of other people, wait with bated breath for each issue.

When Miller took over the storytelling chores on *Daredevil*, it went from being one of Marvel's least-selling books to one of its most popular. Marvel is still making money off Miller's run on the series two decades later.

I recently had drinks with a Hollywood agent at a major agency. We got into a little debate. He kept saying that good films are hard to make; otherwise everyone would be doing it. That sounds good, except I rarely meet practitioners of story who have bothered to do any real study of their craft. They try to reinvent the wheel every time. Or they use a formula that only concentrates on the Iron elements of the story because they perceive that is what audiences really respond to. Or they write something that only uses the Silk elements of the story and then curse the audience for not responding.

The fact is, some storytellers throughout history have been able to have repeated success during their lives, and their stories live beyond their own limited lifespans.

How is this possible? They must be using methods that allow them to speak deeply to a large group of people across culture and time. They were able to repeat their successes, and if you learn their techniques, you stand a better chance of doing so yourself.

In the summer of 2003, the studios were baffled when they released a slew of sequels and franchise films that made much less at the box office than expected.

According to *The New York Times*: "The Hulk, director Ang Lee's eagerly anticipated version of that comic book saga, opened robustly on June 20 (a $62.1 million opening weekend); ticket sales plummeted 70 percent in its second weekend."

Another film expected to do well that summer was *Charlie's Angels: Full Throttle*.

Also, from that same *New York Times* article: "'The Charlie's Angels case is a fascinating one, because it had all the earmarks of being a phenomenal success,' said David Davis, an entertainment analyst for Houlihan, Lokey, Howard and Zukin, an investment banking firm. 'A very expensive marketing spend, all of the stars doing publicity—it had everything going for it. I don't know, maybe after so many of these kind of movies so many weekends in a row, it was just one weekend too many.'"

Most all of these summer films were a disappointment to the studios that made and released them and to the audiences that saw them. Notice how the analyst does not mention the quality of the film's story when he speculates on the film's poor reception.

That same summer, Pixar once again had a huge hit on their hands with *Finding Nemo*.

The good folks at Pixar are almost exclusively concerned with story. They will work on a scene for months, only to throw it out if it doesn't enhance the story. And they have, at the time of my writing this book, nothing but hit films under their belts. Further making my point, *Finding Nemo* went on to become the highest-selling DVD of all time.

I have a friend who was in the story department of another production company. Their job was to come up with feature film ideas to be done using computer graphics. This was after *Shrek* had become a huge hit. My friend told me that he was told not to mention the Toy Story movies as a reference point in his story pitches to studios, because those were considered old. Shrek was what people wanted to see!

The thing that most people don't understand is that well-crafted stories never go out of style. One generation after another has been entertained by Walt Disney's version of *Snow White*—a film originally released in the 1930s.

The 1939 version of *The Wizard of Oz* still enthralls adults and children alike.

A film or book can be a hit for many reasons—timing, new technology, hip language. But only one thing makes a classic—a good story that speaks to the truth of being human.

This is not invisible ink; it is clear to see for anyone who bothers to look. Telling good stories and telling them well can be good business as well as being good for the world that consumes them.

CHAPTER X

My Own Process

- *White Face*
- Tell them what you told them

Following is the screenplay for my short film *White Face*. When I set out to make this film, I was told by those in the know that short films do not make money. There are few venues for them. The film got distribution, makes money, and shows no sign of slowing down.

Here's what I'd like you to do: Read the script twice. The first time, just read it without thinking too much about structure. Just get a feel for it. On the second read, see how much invisible ink you can find.

WHITE FACE
by Brian McDonald
This Draft 10/27/99
©Angry Young Man Prod.

An X-RAY on a light-board. TWO VOICES off-screen discuss the patient's condition. Their language is highly technical and difficult to understand. Fingers point out different areas of the x-ray.

PULL BACK TO REVEAL INT. HOSPITAL-DAY.

TWO DOCTORS in blue surgical scrubs. One of them wears full CLOWN MAKE-UP and a stethoscope around his neck. As the two doctors continue to confer with one another, none of the passersby seem to take notice that one of them is a clown. Their talk is sober, and this is serious business.

     CLOWN DOCTOR (V.O.)
  I'm not going to sit here and tell you it was
  easy to get here.

EXT. HOSPITAL—LATER.

The CLOWN DOCTOR sits on a bench outside the hospital. He speaks to an off-camera interviewer. A caption reads:

  Dr. Howard Blinky.

     CLOWN DOCTOR (CONT'D)
  But I mean it's hard for everybody, right?
  I never thought being a clown would hold me
  back—I just didn't let it stand in my way. Sure
  there are the usual "Bozo" jokes. I've even had
  patients refuse to let me operate on them because
  I'm a clown. That's true. That's absolutely true.
  I remember this one woman kept yelling: "Don't
  touch me—get me a real doctor." Can you believe
  that? In this day and age.
(beat; shrugs)
  I'm good with kids, though.

EXT. MECHANIC'S GARAGE—DAY.

A MIDDLE-AGED CLOWN smokes a cigarette and stands talking to the off-screen interviewer. He wears a greasy jumpsuit and holds an alternator. His caption reads: Ed Yuk-Yuk.

In the background another CLOWN MECHANIC is working under the hood of a car.

> ED YUK-YUK
> (New York accent)
> Well, I grew up in an all-clown neighborhood in the Bronx.

INSERT: A photo of a New York residential street in the '40s. Instead of "normal" people, the streets are populated by clowns.

> ED YUK-YUK (V.O.) (CONT'D)
> I moved out here after I got out of the Marine Corps. After Nam.

INSERT: An old photo of Ed and his Marine buddies.

> ED YUK-YUK (V.O.) (CONT'D)
> Over there nobody cared if you were a clown or not. Every now and then some smart-ass would think it was funny to spray you with a seltzer bottle.

Ed holds up his fist.

> ED YUK-YUK
> Nobody ever did that crap more'n once.

INT. OLD CLOWN WOMAN'S HOUSE—DAY.

The house is decorated with all types of CLOWN FAMILY PHOTOS as well as Circus knick-knacks and statuettes. The OLD CLOWN WOMAN walks out of her kitchen with a cup of hot tea. She talks to the off-screen interviewer.

OLD CLOWN WOMAN

When my parents got here from the old country it was a real bad place for clowns. People would point at them and laugh everywhere they went. It was awful. Just awful.

The woman sits. Her caption reads: Mrs. Clarabelle Confetti.

INSERT: Old black-and-white film footage of signs in windows: "NO CLOWNS ALLOWED" and another which reads: "CLOWNS NEED NOT APPLY."

CLARABELLE

You see, in those days the only way to get out of the old country was to join the circus. That's how our people got associated with the circus, don't you know.

INT. COLLEGE PROFESSOR'S OFFICE—DAY.

This interview takes place in front of the proverbial bookshelves. His caption reads: Barnum N. Bailey Ph.D. Professor of Clown studies. He talks over his half-glasses.

PROF. BAILEY

So what you had happen around the end of the nineteenth century is that clowns became very popular in entertainment. And, to cash in on that, non-clown people began to put on make-up to make themselves appear to be clowns. They would have red rubber noses that they could strap on and they would perform in white-face.

INSERT: Old shot of clowns performing.

> PROF. BAILEY (V.O)
>
> As these fake shows became more popular, the real Clowns were pushed out of the business.

BACK TO PROF. BAILEY.

> PROF. BAILEY
>
> There was so much prejudice at that time that audiences would rather pay to see someone pretending to be a clown instead of the real people.

Depression footage of HOBO CLOWNS.

> PROF. BAILEY (V.O.)
>
> This is where we get the stereotype of the "Hobo Clown." "Hobo" is a very common name in the old country. In America, however, it has become a synonym for "Bum."

BACK TO PROF. BAILEY.

> PROF. BAILEY (CONT'D)
>
> Well, really, look at our entire language. Everything associated with being a clown has negative connotations. I dare anyone watching this show to go to work tomorrow morning and call their boss "a damn Clown" to his face. Or call someone a Bozo—see if you don't get your lights turned out.

EXT. MIDDLE SCHOOL PARKING LOT—DAY.

Dr. Blinky arms his car alarm with his key chain remote and walks away from his BMW. The camera follows close behind. Again the doctor talks to the unseen interviewer.

> CLOWN DOCTOR
> I got called away from the hospital—my son got into another fight…kids.

INT. MIDDLE SCHOOL OFFICE—SHORTLY.

The Doctor approaches the desk and talks to the non-clown SECRETARY behind the desk.

> CLOWN DOCTOR
> Yeah, I'm here about my son. I'm—
> SECRETARY (interrupts; nodding)
> —Cameron's father. I could tell—he's got your nose.

> CLOWN DOCTOR
> (sincere)
> Really.

INT. PRINCIPAL'S OFFICE.

Visibly upset, the Doctor is led, by the non-clown PRINCIPAL, into her office where CAMERON is waiting. The young clown sits pouting in a chair, his arms folded. The boy is dressed like any other child his age.

> PRINCIPAL
> I'm sorry I had to have you come down here again—Cameron can't seem to stay out of trouble.

The Doctor lets out a nose-sigh and then speaks to his son.

> DR. BLINKY
>
> What happened?

The boy shrugs.

> DR. BLINKY (CONT'D)
>
> Look, I can't leave work every time you decide to get into a fight.
> Now you are going to tell me what happened. You know, one more fight and you're expelled. Expelled. You're not going to tell me again that these boys are picking on you for no reason—you must be doing something.
> (to the Principal) What happened?

> PRINCIPAL
>
> Well, you know how boys are. He and two other boys were clowning around—

> DR. BLINKY (interrupts)
>
> —Whoa, whoa, wait a sec—I don't appreciate that kind of—

> PRINCIPAL
>
> —I didn't mean it the way it sounded. It's just an expression. I thought that you people were supposed to have a sense of humor.

> DR. BLINKY
>
> I don't care how you meant it. Look, you know what, don't worry about expelling him. I'm taking him out of here. Cameron, get your jacket.

BACK IN THE PARKING LOT—SHORTLY.

> Dr. Blinky stands next to his car, angry and upset. He is a little ashamed that the camera has caught him in this very candid moment. Massaging the bridge of his nose, he holds back his tears of frustration. After a few moments he speaks. He looks up to reveal the TEARS drawn on his face.

>> DR. BLINKY
> I'm sorry…I—I don't mean to cry… it's just that you work hard all your—I'm a Doctor, for god's sake! Do you have any idea how rare that is—a Clown Doctor—even in this day and age? I work hard, damn hard, so my kids won't have to go through the same shi—crap. I can't believe these attitudes still exist. I went to Harvard!

Cameron, now wearing his jacket, approaches the car. He also sports quite big floppy shoes. They can be heard slapping the pavement.

INT. COLLEGE PROFESSOR'S OFFICE—DAY.

Prof. Bailey addresses the interviewer.

>> PROF. BAILEY
> Many people erroneously believe that things have changed because of certain celebrity Clowns. And, indeed, some Clowns have done quite well for themselves—many by playing up offensive circus stereotypes. Ronald McDonald and Bozo for example.

I honestly don't know how they sleep at night.

EXT. ED YUK-YUK'S–DAY.

Near a car with its hood open, the Clown mechanic is involved in a heated discussion with a customer.

> CUSTOMER
>
> …But how do I know they needed to be replaced?
>
> ED YUK-YUK
>
> You want to see your old parts—I can show you the old parts. (Calling to a Clown in the shop) Rollo, bring out the old parts.
>
> CUSTOMER
>
> I'm just saying I bring it in for a tune-up and you tell me it needs all this extra work. How am I supposed to—
>
> ED YUK-YUK
>
> —What extra work, we just replaced the spark plugs. That's a normal thing to do with a tune-up.

ROLLO arrives with a shallow box containing spark plugs and shows them to the customer, who is a little embarrassed and tries to cover up.

> CUSTOMER
>
> Yeah, but how do I know that those are my old plugs?
>
> ED YUK-YUK (to Rollo)
>
> Are those the man's plugs?

Rollo answers, not by talking but by HONKING his BICYCLE HORN a few times. This is the last straw for the customer.

> CUSTOMER
> Great. This one doesn't even speak English. I try to help you people out, give you a little business, and you try and cheat me.

The customer has been caught being a bigot on film, so he explains his position right into the camera.

> CUSTOMER (CONT'D)
> Look, I'm not prejudiced or anything; it's just that if you're gonna come to this country I think you should learn to speak American. It's for their own good. Besides, who knows what they're talking about? They could be talking about you right in front of your face and you wouldn't even know it.

(Back to Ed)

> What do I owe you? I'm going to a real mechanic, one that at least speaks the language!

The mechanic slams the car's hood shut.

> ED YUK-YUK
> I don't want your money. Why don't you just get the hell outta here before you find yourself pulling my size thirty-six shoes outta your ass?

The man gets in his car and backs out into the street. Rollo is pissed off, and he HONKS angrily at the car. The customer HONKS his CAR HORN back at Rollo as his car speeds away.

EXT. ED YUK-YUK'S GARAGE—DAY.

Rollo looks a little sad; he HONKS to the off-screen interviewer as subtitles translate for us. Ed stands next to his cousin; he listens and nods.

> ROLLO'S SUBTITLES
> My cousin used to send me postcards from America; it seemed like a paradise. Home of Ronald McDonald, yes? But this America is no place for Clowns—we cannot all live in a castle with arches of gold like Mr. McDonald's.
>
> CLARABELLE'S HOUSE-DAY.
> She shows some old family photographs to the camera.
>
> CLARABELLE
> …And these are my parents. Here's one of my husband, Chuckles—God rest his soul. Rodeo accident. It'll be nine years in July. He had the most beautiful smile.

Her mood changes as she shows the next few photos. She's a little angry.

> CLARABELLE (CONT'D)
> This is my son Bobo—he married outside the race, don't you know.
> (Whispers, confidentially) His wife is a Mime.

(Normal voice) What made him go out and do something like that I don't know. Those people aren't like us—but it's his life. I'm just glad his father didn't live to see it. It's really the children that I feel sorry for. They won't know if they're Clowns or Mimes. Oh, and his wife, I can't understand one word that woman says.

She mimics being trapped in a box—then suddenly concerned:

              CLARABELLE (CONT'D)

She's not going to see this, is she?

              EXT. PARK BENCH—DAY.

Dr. Blinky sits on a park bench, enjoying an ice cream cone with Cameron. There are no tears drawn on his face. He talks to the interviewer.

              DR. BLINKY

This thing with my son has really made me stop and take a long hard look at that man in the mirror. I thought that a good job, a Beamer and a house in the 'burbs was gonna fix everything. That people would see me as a person first and maybe just plain forget that I'm a Clown.

> (laughs at himself)
>
> I guess the world hasn't changed much since I was a kid—people still think it's funny to make fun of someone who doesn't look like them. Maybe things will be different for my son's generation.

EXT. MECHANIC'S GARAGE—DAY.

Ed the Mechanic Clown stands outside his shop talking to the interviewer.

> MECHANIC CLOWN
>
> I talked my cousin Rollo into staying in this country. Sure it has its problems, but I still think it's the best country in the world. Things are getting better all the time for Clowns. The way things are going, it looks like one day we might even have a Clown in the White House.

INT. COLLEGE PROFESSOR'S OFFICE—DAY.

Prof. Bailey addresses the interviewer.

> PROF. BAILEY
>
> In the end it is incumbent upon those Clowns in powerful positions to educate people about our problems. There are many Clown celebrities who choose to remain "closeted," if you will. These individuals are usually of mixed heritage and with a little make-up can "pass," so to speak, for another, more accepted, race.

> PROF. BAILEY (CONT'D)
> Perhaps some of you watching this film have some clowns in your family tree. You need to stand up and say to America that you are clowns and proud of it!

DISSOLVE TO:

A photo of Clarabelle Confetti against a black background on the left-hand side of the screen. The following captions fade up, on the right and side, in turn.

CAPTIONS

This film is dedicated to the memory of Miss Clarabelle Confetti, who passed away shortly after filming was completed. She was well loved in her community, and her memorial was attended by over one hundred Clowns.

They all arrived in one limousine.

FADE OUT.

When people see *White Face,* they often think it's improvised. Most of the time people enjoy the film, but the structure is invisible to them.

Let's go through the script so that you can see what I was doing.

Notice how I started with Doctor Blinky in a normal setting doing an important job. This is the story's reality. Though this is a comedy, it uses incongruity rather than blatant slapstick or parody for its humor. It is a satire.

Also, the voice-over helps start to define that he is of a "Clown race," not just a guy in clown make-up.

The doctor's personality is defined, too. He is a man determined to overcome any racism in the world through his professional excellence. Not to mention that it reveals racism in this fictional world, and that it will be dealt with in this film.

Ed Yuk-Yuk, the mechanic, is more of a blue-collar guy. This starts to let us see that Clowns occupy various strata of society. Also, creating this tough-guy Clown who has been to Vietnam again says that much of the humor in this story will come out of incongruity. Using 'Nam also grounds the piece in a kind of reality. It says that this is the real world as we know it, but as if Clowns were a race of people; so it reiterates the idea that this story deals with race issues.

Clarabelle Confetti gives us a third perspective on this world. She allows us to see the past prejudices inflicted on Clowns.

These three distinct characters give us what appears to be a cross-section of Clown-America.

The professor is more of a device than a character. He tells the audience things they need to know to understand the story. For instance, when he talks about the negative connotations of the word "Clown," the scene in the principal's office in which the phrase "clowning around" is used follows it. Because of what comes before, we know how to view the insult.

Notice now that the next time we visit each of the characters, a problem is introduced. Conflict. In the case of the doctor, it is his being called into the principal's office of his son's school. The mechanic is confronted by the bigotry of a customer. And the old woman reveals her own prejudice.

When people see the film, they always mention how the film really gets going when the doctor and the principal have their scene together. Of course—it's the first conflict in the film. Conflict keeps people interested. But Act 2 only works because of Act 1. Act 1 becomes the invisible ink that makes the rest of the film work.

The doctor is often regarded as the main character. It is because he's the character of change in the story. In the second act his belief system is challenged. It's more than just something funny happening.

Each character has three acts. The second act for the mechanic is when he has a run-in with the bigoted customer. Through his intro in Act 1, we know that Ed Yuk-Yuk is an American who grew up in the Bronx and fought for his country. So we understand how deeply the insult cuts when he is accused of cheating a customer.

With Clarabelle, the conflict is her own bigotry. She thinks it's her son's choice of a wife, but we know differently. How do we know? We know this because we have established a reality in which racists are bad people whose hatred can hurt others. Never mind that most of us believe that this is true in life; what is important is that it is dramatized by the story.

Act 3 is tricky to see in these stories because it appears to be a part of Act 2.

With Doctor Blinky, Act 3 is the scene at his car where he cries and we see the reaction to his experience.

In the mechanic's story, Rollo, the horn-honking Clown, is a less defined character and is more the internal voice of Ed. Is this country everything he thought it would be? Ed's beliefs are challenged here. The scene with Rollo's speech is that story's Act 3.

Clarabelle's death is a combination Act 3 and dénouement ("Ever since that day"). How does her story resolve itself? She dies. What is her "Ever since that day"? She dies. And you can bet her racist attitudes remained with her for the rest of her life. She did not change.

Doctor Blinky's dénouement? We can see in his last scene how he has changed. He is not the same person he was at the story's start. He has grown through the ritual pain of being confronted with racist viewpoints he had spent years denying. His son is a clone—a view of the doctor's past. Seeing how these attitudes affect his son is what forces him to change.

The story has a three-act structure, but most people don't see that it's there. It is invisible to them. I had a producer from a major star's production company call me after he had seen the film. He wanted to know if I would be interested in working with them, but first he wanted to see something that would show that I understood narrative.

Understand that he loved the movie. He said he thought it was brilliant, but he couldn't tell if I could tell a story. He knew nothing of invisible ink.

TELL THEM WHAT YOU TOLD THEM

I wasn't sure how to end this book until I gave it to a friend to read and she told me that she enjoyed the book because she and I share the same taste in films. I knew then that I had failed to get my point across. This is not about personal taste.

The idea that one could view a story through the lens of objectivity is so foreign to some that they don't even know it is a possibility. But if you are to master this craft, that is what you must strive to do.

When you read a sentence and find a misspelled word or grammar mistake, do you think for an instant that it might just be your opinion? You probably don't. That's because you understand the language and its rules. When you are speaking with someone who has only rudimentary skills in your language, you can tell immediately, just as you will soon be able to do with the language of drama.

One of your tasks as a storyteller is to understand that the language of story has its own rules of grammar and syntax. If you were watching *The Wizard of Oz* and, in it, they decided the idea should be Dorothy's about how to get the apples from the trees; and then they had Tin Man come up with other plans; and at the end of the story, they said it was Scarecrow who had the brains all along—it would all be bad grammar. It would be a mistake, and you would know it.

Drama is a language, and its principles can be observed, learned, and executed. One way to master this skill is to try to understand what you respond to in a story. Ask yourself if you are having a personal reaction to something outside the story. If you abhor violence in stories and you read a book that has violence in it, ask yourself if it is there to support the story's armature.

Conversely, if you enjoy violence, ask yourself the same question. Is it necessary for the story to be told this way? If the story were *The Godfather*, then the answer would be yes. If the story is *Toy Story*, then the answer is probably no.

Ask yourself this question about dialogue, costumes, scenery, photography, religion, language, personal philosophy, politics, a particular actor or actress, special effects, genre, music, and any other element that might find its way into a story. You will have strong feelings about some of these things, and it will distort your view of a story.

I once had a student tell me that she hated *E.T.* because of the swearing. Most of us would be hard-pressed to remember any swearing in the film, but it was enough to ruin the film for her. Many of us do this kind of thing. We will love or hate something in a story for reasons outside the story itself.

We must take ourselves out of the equation if we are ever to learn to see and use story structure. This is not easy, but it is possible to do. To do this, you may have to suffer the ritual pain of letting go of some of the things you hold dear. If you go to see films because of the special effects, you must not let them cloud your judgment about the quality of the piece. Ask yourself if the story has resonance for those who care little for special effects or photography or your favorite actor. Does it have an armature, and does every element in the story contribute to dramatizing that armature? To do this effectively, you may have to die as the writer you are in order to be reborn. When you do it, many things that are now muddy in your mind will become clear. You will ascend.

You will see the footprints in the grass.

Books by Brian McDonald

One of **Brian McDonald's** favorite childhood memories is sitting on the front porch with his family, watching movies from a nearby drive-in theater. This early fascination with storytelling and filmmaking stayed with him, as his mother recalled there was never a time when Brian wasn't interested in stories. Despite struggling with dyslexia and doubting his ability to write professionally, Brian found motivation in bookstores, believing that all the authors couldn't be smarter than him.

Today, as an award-winning director, writer, and author, Brian is proud of overcoming these difficulties to pursue his passion for storytelling. He loves watching classic movies and feels the profound responsibility of being a storyteller, especially when fans share how his work has helped them through difficult times.

◉

Unlock the power of storytelling with Brian McDonald through keynote speeches, writing workshops, story seminars, and panel discussions.

FEATURED CLIENTS:

Disney | Pixar | Sony | Cirque du Soleil | Lucasfilm | Microsoft
Respawn Entertainment | Visa | Ford | Future of Storytelling

To check Brian's availability for speaking, consulting and directing please contact:
Sweetwood Creative
info@sweetwoodproductions.com

For more insights listen to Brian's award-winning podcasts
You Are a Storyteller and
You Are a Storyteller: Masters at the Craft.
https://writeinvisibleink.com

www.ingramcontent.com/pod-product-compliance
Lightning Source LLC
Chambersburg PA
CBHW031319160426
43196CB00007B/585